Praise for

"Yong Kang's passion is an inspiration – animation's gain is undoubtedly accountancy's loss!"

– Steve Burton, EVP of HBO Asia

"You have been warned. Reading *Fearless Passion* may make you quit your uninspiring job right now. If you feel trapped in your current job, this book is what you need."

– Bobby Beck, CEO and co-founder of Animation Mentor

"*Fearless Passion* is fun yet emotional; creative yet logical; entertaining yet informative. You get the best of both worlds. No matter what genre of self-help you prefer, I'm sure you'll relate to this book."

– Drew McKevitt, creator of Angry Pear

"Yong Kang shares a fresh perspective on how to handle the fear of not having enough money in *Fearless Passion*, and explains why passion should not be ignored."

– John Lee Dumas, founder of EntrepreneurOnFire.com

"This clear, easy-to-follow book will guide you to your passion and inspire you to follow it!"

– Lauren Kristen, CEO of Kristen Development Corp.

"The happiest people I know devote a lot of energy to their passions. I agree with Yong Kang — it's essential to make time to develop your skills and interests. Passion is what makes life worth living. This book will help you figure out your passions and give yourself permission to pursue them."

– Martha Bullen, publishing consultant and coauthor of
Turn Your Talents into Profits

"Fearless Passion is written in a simple but intimate style that inspires. Throughout the book Yong Kang's enthusiasm and belief in following your passions shines clearly through. It's not a book you'll want to miss."

– Vivien Fock, home Tutor

"With authenticity and simplicity, Yong Kang busts 8 myths on passion and offers insights on overcoming fears so you can realize your dreams and fulfill your destiny. Read this book and get ready to live your passion!"

– Master Phil Nguyen, author of
*Bully Buster & Beyond! 9 Treasures to
Self-Confidence, Self-Esteem, and Strength of Character*

FEARLESS PASSION

Find the Courage to Do What You Love

YONG KANG CHAN

Fearless Passion: Find the Courage to Do What You Love
Copyright © 2014 by Yong Kang Chan

Printed in the United States of America

First Edition, 2014

ISBN 978-981-09-1414-1

Cover designed by Yong Kang Chan
Cover photo from iStockphoto / RichVintage
Author photo by Benson Ang
Book edited by Madalyn Stone

*To everyone out there who feels trapped
in their current jobs or are
searching for meaningful work they love.*

CONTENTS

Preface: Why Did I Write this Book?   *ix*

Introduction: Why I Divorced My Job   *xi*

Part 1: Understanding Passion

1   Why Passion Matters to You   3

2   The Eight Biggest Myths on Passion You Need to   15
    Bust

Part 2: Understanding Fear

3   What Is Stopping You from Realizing Your   47
    Dreams?

4   The Greatest Fear: Not Having Enough Money   61

5   Other Hidden Fears You Need to Uncover   77

6   How to Harness Your Fears   102

Part 3: Acting on Your Passion

7   How to Identify What You Love to Do   125

8   What to Do When You Have Many Passions   150

9   Use Passions to Build the Skills You Want   173

10 How to Bring Your Passion to Work   189

11 Be Prepared before You Change Careers   202

12 How to Be Passionate beyond Work   235

Final Thoughts   247

Acknowledgments   249

Story Contributors   251

About the Author   255

Preface

WHY DID I WRITE THIS BOOK?

FIRST, WRITING IS ONE OF MY PASSIONS! You can read more about my passion for writing in chapter 9. More importantly, I want to inspire others to do what they love because getting stuck doing something you don't care about is not a good place for anyone. I know this firsthand.

For years, I have heard people around me say:

- They don't have passion.
- They don't have enough skills to do what they love as their career.
- It's not possible to make a living with your passion.
- They're not as brave as I was.
- You can do it because you are multitalented.

This book explains what passion is and clears away misconceptions like these statements regarding passion. To me, I feel that:

- Everyone has passion.

- You can develop skills to do what you love as a career.
- It's definitely possible to make a living with your passion.
- I'm just as fearful as you are, but you don't have to let fears stop you from taking action.
- I'm not multi talented; I'm just multi passionate.

Each chapter begins with a real-life story to inspire you to take action. A few of them are mine, while others are contributed by passionate people I have interviewed. At the end of each story, there's also a key message box like the one in the introduction.

People tend to label what is good or bad in their life. But I feel that all life events have meaningful lessons behind them. My choice of a career I disliked could have been seen as a bad experience. However, if I didn't pick the wrong career, I wouldn't have known how to pick the right career for me and pursue my passion professionally. And then I wouldn't be writing this book.

All experiences help us grow.

The stories in this book will give you the courage to do what you love.

So let's get going!

Introduction

WHY I DIVORCED MY JOB

IN 2008, I GRADUATED AS A LOST SHEEP from Nanyang Technological University (NTU). Even with a bachelor's degree in accounting, I had no idea what job to pursue. The "Big Four" audit firms came to my university to prey on new graduates, and like a sheep, I blindly joined one of them, KPMG.

Actually, I knew from the start that my passion wasn't in accounting. I enjoy being creative and have loved the media industry since I was a child. I wanted to get into mass communications in university, but unfortunately, I didn't do well enough on my General Paper to qualify. So, after eliminating all the courses I didn't want to take, I was left with accounting.

In my three years of study, I nevertheless continued to develop my passions. While my friends took finance electives, I took music and movie electives. But it never occurred to me that one day I would pursue my passion as my job. Everyone around me said it was too difficult to find a good job in the creative field and I should just keep my passion as a hobby. It was only when I started working as an auditor in KMPG that I

xii Yong Kang Chan

had an epiphany:

> *"Why am I doing a job I don't like? I spend most of my waking hours working. Do I really want to spend one-third of my life doing something I hate?"*

I never enjoyed being an auditor, and it wasn't the long working hours or stressful deadlines. I just **couldn't find any meaning** in the job. I couldn't find the reason to wake up early in the morning to go to work. I didn't want to spend one-third of my life in a job that made me unhappy and another one-third of my life trying to make myself happy.

Why Don't I Just Be Happy?

I remember one day I was at my client's office and the thought of switching on my laptop made me want to cry. I knew it was just a job. My parents told me to bear with it. But to force myself to do something I disliked made me feel trapped and powerless. It was killing my soul every day. The moment when I saw my colleague run into the ladies room in tears, I knew that enough was enough. I had to end my unhappy relationship with auditing.

Not wanting to get another job I hated, I began to consider my passions as career options. Therefore:

- I read books and articles online on changing careers and passions.
- I took personality tests to find out what jobs would suit me.

- I went to job fairs to see what jobs were available in the creative industry.

One day, as I was reading the book *What Color Is Your Parachute?* by Richard N. Bolles, I had an idea. The book states that you can change a career in two steps by first changing your industry and then changing the nature of your job, or vice versa. First, I could be an accountant in the media industry and then find a creative job. So I started compiling a list of all the media companies in Singapore. And regardless of whether the companies were hiring or not, I sent in my resume.

Without knowing what passion to pursue as a career, I divorced auditing and worked as an accountant in HBO Asia for another three years. Today, I'm dating animation. And although I only knew that animation was a possible career option in 2009, it had been one of my passions since way back.

Passion Reveals Itself to You

Who knew a movie could have so much impact on my life? In 2003, I watched an animated film by Pixar called *Finding Nemo*. This movie has a very special place in my heart. It's one of the earliest animations I watched in the cinema. Not only is the film funny and touching, the relationship between the father clown fish (Marlin) and his son (Nemo) reminds me so much of my relationship with my dad.

In the movie, Marlin is overly protective toward his only son, Nemo. He constantly warns his son about the danger of the ocean and worries that he will get hurt. It is the same for my dad. And being the "Nemo" that I was growing up, I always liked to challenge what my dad said I couldn't do (including pursuing my passion).

After *Finding Nemo*, I started watching more animation and soon fell in love with this art form. But I didn't know I could be an animator in Singapore.

Inspiration only Came to Me when I Was Shopping

One lucky day in 2009 while I was shopping in Marina Square, I stumbled upon this creative industry fair. And I must have behaved like a kid in a candy store, taking all the brochures I could get, feeling so excited and happy. All the jobs and courses were so interesting to me. When I reached the animation section, I paused for a second and thought to myself:

"There are schools in Singapore that teach animation? There are studios here that actually make animation?"

The creative fair was an eye-opener for me. I came from an accounting background and had zero knowledge about animation except for watching it. I wasn't even aware that I could learn animation. Like many others, I didn't know how animation was made. My impression was that the animators needed to draw very well. And although I liked to draw, I couldn't draw images like those seen in *The Lion King* and *Beauty and the Beast*. No way! What I didn't know is you don't need to be good in drawing to be an animator.

Deciding to Be an Animator

After attending the creative fair again the next year, I visited one of the local animation schools called CG Protégé in 2011. The school director, David Kwok, was very kind and explained the three different areas in animation to me: character animation, visual effects, and modeling. While he was explaining them, I knew straightaway I wanted to study character animation because acting is required and I love acting. That day, I found my passion in character animation.

For those who don't know what passion is, it goes something like this:

> You get all excited and pumped up just by listening to someone describing the scope of the job to you. In your mind, you are like, 'Yes, yes, yes, that's what I want to do!' You feel like you can do anything. You're full of energy. And you just want to start right away. That's passion in a nutshell.

Once I decided to be an animator and committed to it, everything else just fell into place. I found a perfect place to develop my craft—an online school in California called Animation Mentor. I discovered self-help books, audio programs, and websites that provided me with the courage to pursue what I love. I began to meet other passionate people and people who were supportive of my dreams.

Fast forward to today: I've recently graduated from Animation Mentor and I'm looking forward to working in the animation industry.

Key Lessons from My Story

1. Pay attention to what you love to do.

Don't worry how your passion is going to play a part in your life. Just be aware of what you love to do. You will know what your passion is for when the times come.

I watched animation because I loved it. I never thought I would pursue it as a career one day. But because I knew what I loved and understood myself well, I took a closer look at the creative fair. And if I didn't know I loved acting, I wouldn't have known instantly that character animation was right for me when I heard the job description.

2. Knowing what your passion is helps you connect the dots.

Your passion might not look grand or useful to you right now, but be open and receptive to inspiration. You don't know how your passion might lead you to bigger things in the future.

3. Passion evolves faster when you take action on it.

An animation inspired me in 2003. It took six years before I realized it was possible to make a living out of it, two years to clarify my passion, and another two years to develop the skills. That is a total of ten years!

My passion for watching animation slowly evolved into a passion for doing character animation only when I took action and visited a school. If I had taken the time to do research on the animation industry initially, it wouldn't have taken me six years to know that an animator job existed. And it wouldn't have taken me another two years to find out what character animation is. So, find out more about your passion now.

4. Decisions move you forward.

Five years ago, when I decided I had enough of auditing, I just left my job without another job. Decisions make you take action. I could have wavered because of my fears. But once you make a decision to do something and commit to it, everything else that doesn't align with it just doesn't matter to you anymore.

5. Once you decide to do something, things will start to fall into place naturally.

Making a decision is powerful. Not long after I decided to leave my job, I stumbled upon the creative fair. And soon after I decided to find an accounting job in the media industry, I saw an opening in HBO Asia.

After the school visit, I made another decision. I committed ten years of my life from September 2011 to August 2021 to do animation and be a great character animator. I wrote down my commitment in my journal and signed it. Again, things started to change for me. Resources that I didn't know previously existed—such as online animation schools and self-help podcasts—started to appear.

Life will take care of itself. You just need to make a decision and commit to it.

PART 1:
UNDERSTANDING PASSION

Chapter 1

WHY PASSION MATTERS TO YOU

"WHAT? FOUR DAYS IN A THEME PARK?" You must be kidding!"

This was my first thought when my friends suggested we should spend at least four days in Walt Disney World for our trip to the United States last year. I mean, I love Disney cartoons. I love Mickey Mouse. In fact, I was studying character animation online, but isn't Disney World for kids? How would a twenty-nine-year-old guy like me survive four full days in Disneyland without being bored?

To my surprise, Walt Disney World turned out to be one of the highlights of my US trip. I remember that on our third day there, it was pouring rain. I took shelter in one of the attractions called, "One Man's Dream." It's a gallery that depicts Walt Disney's life through words, photos, artifacts, and so on.

At the end of the walkthrough gallery, there's this fifteen-minute video showing Walt Disney himself recount his story, challenges, and dream. I felt touched and inspired watching it. I grew up watching Disney's cartoons but it was only at that moment that I felt a connection to Walt Disney.

"The way to get started is to quit talking and begin doing." — Walt Disney

There are three main reasons why I wanted to share this story:

1. Passion played a huge part in Walt's success.

Walt faced a number of obstacles in his career:

- His earlier company, Laugh-O-Grams, went bankrupt.
- He had to abandon his successful character, Oswald the Lucky Rabbit, because his distributor owned the rights to the character.
- A few of his early films, such as *Pinocchio* and *Fantasia*, were not commercially successful.
- In 1941, Walt Disney Studios' animators went on a labor strike.
- It took him more than twenty years to acquire the rights to *Mary Poppins* from the author, P. L. Travers.

Despite all these obstacles, he still persisted so he could create his dream theme park, Disneyland. He could have given up along the way, but his passions for family, entertainment, animation, and storytelling kept him going.

2. Passion needs to be supported by action.

Through Walt Disney, I've learned that to conjure up something magical, you need both passion and action.

> **Even magic needs work, too.**
> **It doesn't happen by a swing of the wand.**
>
> Life is like a set of puzzle pieces. It takes several puzzle pieces to form the picture you want. Passion alone will not lead you to success. It is only one of the many pieces in the puzzle. It is definitely a key piece, but you still have to do the work and piece the puzzle together.
>
> **3. Passion comes from the heart, not the mind.**
> Your mind can't tell you what you love. Only your heart can. My mind told me that I wouldn't enjoy Disneyland because I was too old for it. That wasn't true.
>
> The mind and the heart serve different purposes. The mind is used to rationalize while the heart is used to love. You can think of all the things that you want in life and justify why they are important to you. But without the emotional input from your heart, there's always something missing and you feel unfulfilled.
>
> So, don't figure out what your passion is using your mind. Open your heart, and let it guide you to your passion.

What Is Passion?

Passion is when your fire dies out and you still want to keep going. When the initial enthusiasm for doing something is over, but you are still in love with doing that something—that's passion!

The Word "Leap" Describes Passion the Best

There is no better way to describe passion than the word "leap":

- When you are passionate about something, you want to *leap* out of your bed every morning and do it.
- Doing what you love is like *leaping* for joy.
- Sometimes, pursuing passion feels like taking a *leap* of faith when you are uncertain of what it will bring you.
- Other times, pursuing passion can bring quantum *leaps* to your career and life.

Figure 1.1 I was doing a *Book of Mormon* leap at Central Park after watching the musical for a second time.

More importantly, passion possesses four elements that form the word "leap":

Love

Energy

Authenticity

Purpose

They help to explain why passion matters.

Passion Is Love

Passion is simply doing what you love to do. It can be as simple as watching your favorite TV program or as noble as serving the nation. It doesn't matter.

What matters is commitment. When you truly love something, you give it the attention and care it deserves. You take actions to help it grow. These actions are genuinely what you desire to do. They are not obligations.

You Have the Choice When It Comes to Love; Make Yourself Happy

Pursuing your passion is joyous. Fulfilling what your heart desires makes you happy.

When you love something, your perception differs from someone who doesn't love what he's doing. You see pursuing your passion as interesting and fun. You put in your time and effort voluntarily because you enjoy every second of it. It's worthwhile to you.

Someone who doesn't love what he does thinks pursuing passion is tough work he has to do to get what he wants. To him, it is a chore instead of play. He doesn't get it.

Give Yourself Courage

I love this quote by Lao-Tzu:

> *"Being deeply loved by someone gives you strength, while loving someone deeply gives you courage."*

It applies to passion, too. When you love what you do deeply, it gives you the courage to overcome your fears.

Pursuing passion brings out a lot of fears you have. You might be unsure of how to pursue your passion. You might be afraid that you cannot support yourself with your passion. You might be worried about losing the things you have now.

But when your passion is strong, your fears appear small in comparison. They just become opportunities for you to be brave.

Create a Positive Environment

My brother used to have a job that he disliked. Every time he came back home, he would share with me all the things he didn't like about his job. I felt drained just listening to his complaints!

After he left his job and started doing what he loved, the mood of our conversation changed. There is more laughter; the vibe he exudes is more positive.

Doing what you love creates a positive environment. It allows you to spend quality time with your family. Focusing on the negative aspects of your work, on the other hand, takes you out of the present. It brings you back to work and distracts you from bonding with your family.

Passion Is Energy

What do you see when you see a passionate person talk?

You see someone who is excited and has a lot to share. It feels like the person is ignited with enthusiasm and ready to do something.

Passion gives you energy to get started and keep taking actions. I call it "Passion Energy." It is different from physical energy. You can be physically tired but still feel energized and pumped up to do what you love.

"Passion Energy" Makes You More Persistent

"Passion Energy" is an additional source of energy to you. It is the voice that encourages you to keep trying when you face an obstacle. It is the force that drives you forward through all the challenges.

Those who don't like what they do fail to benefit from this extra energy source. They have to depend on external motivations like money to push them forward toward their goals.

Work Long Hours without Feeling Tired

How do you feel at the end of the day doing something you hate?

You feel exhausted and drained, don't you?

Why?

Because you are using a lot of your physical, mental, and emotional energy to force yourself to do work you hate. Your personal energy is wasted in resisting your job. It takes more effort this way.

When you love what you do, you have "passion energy." Less energy is required of you. It explains why passionate people can do something they love for hours and hours without feeling tired at all.

No Need for Discipline Anymore

Some friends asked me how I have the discipline to study animation and hand in weekly assignments when I have a full-time job.

The answer is simple. I love to do animation.

Most of my classmates can cope with their animation studies, too despite working full-time. A few of them even have families to take care of. But all of us can manage because we are passionate about animation. We want to create good animation.

When you enjoy doing what you do, you feel motivated and just want to do more of it. Discipline is not required to keep you on track.

Passion Is Authenticity

What does passion feel like?

It feels like you are a paper clip being attracted to a magnet; your passion is pulling you toward it—it's effortless. You don't have to do anything else other than the thing you love. It feels natural to you.

On the other hand, doing something you hate is like forcing a screw into a hole that doesn't fit or trying to get two repelling sides of the magnets to connect together. It doesn't work.

Give Yourself the Freedom to Be Yourself

Doing what you love is the best way of saying
"I love you" to yourself.

Doing what you love means you are being true to yourself. It means you love yourself. You accept who you are and what you love. You give yourself permission to do what you desire.

You are not allowing yourself to be who you are when you do something you dislike. You feel trapped and unnatural. It hurts you in the long run, not just spiritually but also adversely affects your health.

Connect with Others Easily

Your passion reflects who you are. It helps others to get to know you quicker and relate to you better.

If you are a quiet person like me, sharing what you love is definitely a good conversation starter. It allows the other party to come up with interesting questions to ask you and that eases social awkwardness.

Also, you are more natural when you talk about your passion. You shift your focus from your ability to interact with others to what you love. It takes the pressure off you as a speaker and it becomes much easier to make small talk with others.

Attract Like-Minded People

Pursuing passion gives you the opportunity to meet people with similar interests to yours. After I started studying animation online, I began to make friends all over the world with people who love animation as much as I do. We share our work and give each other feedback. I'm also constantly updated with the latest animation news through my friends on social media.

This is only possible when you are true to your passion.

Passion Is Purpose

Imagine driving around the city without a destination in mind. You just keep driving in circles or wherever the road brings you. The only times you stop are when your vehicle runs out of gas or when you need to sleep, eat, or go to the restroom.

This is what it feels like when you're living a life without passion. It doesn't matter where you go. You can go to the mall, the park, or the supermarket. All of the places appear the same to you when you have no purpose in mind. It's only when you have a purpose (such as having to prepare a dinner), then the place (supermarket) will be meaningful to you.

Add Meaning to Life

Passion helps to clarify your life purpose. It makes your life more meaningful and fulfilling. As you do more of what you love, you become more aware of why it is important to you.

Take my passion for writing, for example. At first, I started writing just to express my creativity through words and to encourage myself. As I wrote more and started blogging, I realized that I enjoyed sharing my thoughts and connecting with others. Now that I'm writing this book, my main purpose is to inspire you to pursue your passion.

My purpose becomes clearer the more I do what I love.

Make Decisions Faster

With passion, goals emerge naturally and making decisions becomes easier. If you love to cook, you will be excited to plan what to cook next. If you love to travel, you will plan which country to visit next. **Passion guides you toward what to do next.**

Knowing why you love to do something helps you filter out all other activities that don't align with it. It leaves you with fewer options to choose from, which makes your decision-making process faster.

Save on Time and Resources

Although passion doesn't provide an exact path to reach your goal, it gives you a specific destination that aids you in planning your route.

Knowing where you are heading is more important than knowing the path. There are always many ways to reach a destination. However, if you are unsure of your destination and end up at a place that isn't where you want to go, you will have wasted your time and resources to get there.

Chapter 2

THE EIGHT BIGGEST MYTHS ON PASSION YOU NEED TO BUST

SIMON GUDGEON ONLY STARTED SCULPTING when he was forty years old, but since then, his works have been exhibited internationally in London, New York, San Diego, Paris, and the Netherlands. He has done major public sculptures in his Sculptures by the Lake project as well.

When Simon was young, although he always enjoyed art in school, he didn't know how to become an artist.

There wasn't any obvious career path.

He studied law at Reading University in England—not because he wanted to be a lawyer, but because he didn't know what else to pursue as a career. He thought a law degree would be a good foundation for any profession. However, after spending six years learning to become a qualified lawyer, he knew he didn't want to be a lawyer, and so he never practiced law.

Not knowing what he wanted to do in life, Simon explored several other jobs:

- He exported antique prints to the United States.
- He did commercial photography.
- He did promotional marketing.
- He even started a garden maintenance and landscaping business, which he later expanded into retail, selling garden products. Unfortunately, his business ended during the recession.

Reuniting with Art

When Simon was in his thirties, his mother bought him some paint, and that was when he decided to be an artist. At that time, he was a house-sitter. He had a place to live and didn't have to look for a job for four years. He had the opportunity to paint and draw every day. After putting in many hours and a lot of hard work, he mastered these skills and had a few successful exhibitions.

Although Simon enjoyed painting for the most part, sometimes it was a struggle for him. His painting journey was full of ups and downs. One day, he hit a painting block, and he just couldn't produce anything. So he took a couple of days off to tidy up his studio and get away from his work.

As he was tidying up his studio, he found in one of his cupboards some clay and sculpting tools he had bought some time ago. He had never sculpted before, but sculpture had always fascinated him. That day, he took out the clay and experimented with sculpting. And he was hooked! He absolutely loved the process of translating his ideas into physical objects. There was an indescribable connection he had with sculpting. It just felt right.

Later, he realized it wasn't just the making of the sculpture that he loved; he enjoyed selling and marketing his sculptures, too. That was the turning point of his career. *He knew intuitively that was how he was going to earn his living.*

Passion vs Making Money

There were challenges involved when it came to pursuing sculpting as a career:

- First, there was the challenge of making the sculpture.
- Second, Simon had to judge whether it was worthwhile to make the sculpture.
- Last, he needed to market his work to make a living.

To create a piece of sculpture, Simon had to invest a lot of money, sometimes up to tens of thousands of pounds. And he had to bear all the risks by himself first. He didn't know how the market would respond to his work until he put it out there. He could only depend on his own judgment.

But even so, Simon refused to do commissioned work. Creating what somebody else wants for money didn't inspire him at all. He believed that:

> *You need passion to create the best art*
> *you can possibly create.*

If he didn't feel good about doing the sculpture, he knew it wouldn't turn out well. On the contrary, if he put his enthusiasm and heart into his artwork, the work would be great and people would respond to it. People who really loved his sculptures could then go to one of his exhibitions and buy something they liked.

His bottom line was: **You can't sacrifice art for money.**

To make a living as a sculptor for the past sixteen years, he chose to produce great work and focus on marketing them instead. And from his worldwide success, he proved that this strategy paid off.

Key Lessons from Simon's Story

1. You can always start something new.

Simon didn't start painting until his thirties or sculpting until his forties. Even though he didn't have any formal education in sculpting, that didn't stop him. He just developed his skills by experimenting, putting in countless hours of practice, and learning techniques on the Internet. With his passion, he learned sculpting, painting, and drawing on his own.

It's never too late to learn something new and be good at it. You can pick up almost anything at any time. All you need is passion and an inquiring mind.

2. If you really want to do something, do it.

During my interview with Simon, he said something that I love very much:

**Never regret what you've done;
always regret what you didn't do.**

Simon spent six years in law and although he didn't like it, he didn't dwell on it. He just moved on and continued searching for what he wanted to do in life.

The worst thing you can do with your life is to have regrets about what you didn't do. If you really want to do something, go for it. Don't procrastinate, even if it seems risky, because everything in life is risky. If you want to stay safe, you aren't going to accomplish anything great.

Simon was willing to invest money in his art because he was very committed to sculpting. It provided a lot of meaning in his life. If you are really passionate about something and put in the hours to master it, you can make a living out of it. But you have to commit to it and take risks. **You can't be wishy-washy with your passion.**

3. Marketing is essential today.

Simon mentioned that marketing is hugely important today, even if you are an artist. Thirty years ago, if you went into a gallery and you liked an artist's work, you could only buy it there. There was no way to contact the artist. Artists at that time didn't have to market their work, as the gallery did all the marketing for them.

But now with the Internet, most artists have their own website. Customers can go to their favorite artists' websites and buy their art online. Galleries don't market artists very much anymore because the customers are buying from the artists directly. Thus, **you need to market yourself.**

Simon suggested putting at least half of your time into

> marketing. It's pointless spending 100 percent of your time creating work that no one is going to see.

Don't Follow Your Passion Blindly

Today, I did a Google search on "follow your passion." Guess what? Nine out of ten results on the first page tell you that to "follow your passion" is bad advice. The advice is described as crappy, bizarre, and that it makes you miserable.

I should be angry after reading those articles, but I'm rather amused instead. "Follow your passion" is a phrase of only three words! If anyone were to base a career on just three words, I'd be worried.

"Follow your passion" is definitely good advice; there's nothing wrong with it. The problem comes when people confuse themselves by taking it too literally. "Follow your passion" does not discount the importance of skills, strengths, effort, and so on.

If you have skill, use it.
If you have strength, use it.
If you have passion, make sure you use it!

The advice also doesn't tell you to give up everything you have for your passion. "Follow your passion" **doesn't mean following your passion blindly.**

Love is never blind. You have to open your eyes to opportunities around you as you pursue your passion. The advice merely says there are certain benefits to pursuing your passion. Pursue it if you want to enjoy those benefits.

Plus, "follow your passion" is not the only advice out there. Use as much advice as you need to get what you want in life. Decide what is best for you. Ultimately, you are the decision maker; your passion might push you in one direction, but you are still in control of your choices.

You Give Love a Bad Name

From reading online and talking to others, I have gathered eight major myths people have about passion:

1. I need a passion to start.
2. I need to have talent to do what I love.
3. Pursuing passion makes me selfish.
4. It's too late for me to do what I love.
5. I'm too busy to do what I love.
6. Doing too much of what you love kills the passion.
7. Do what you love and the money will follow.
8. Pursuing passion will make me poor.

Increasingly, there are online comments that passion isn't useful. Unfortunately, these statements come from people who have totally misunderstood passion. With this chapter, I want to provide another perspective on passion. Hopefully, by busting these myths, I can undo some of the criticism about passion.

Here goes!

Myth #1: I Need a Passion to Start

The reason why the advice "follow your passion" doesn't work for most people is because they think they need to find their passion before they can start. The truth is **you don't need a passion to pursue one.**

Needing a passion to start is like needing air to start breathing. You don't need to find oxygen before you can start breathing. You just breathe and oxygen will enter your nostrils naturally. If there isn't any oxygen in the room, you will know it.

Pursuing a passion starts when you decide and commit to doing what you love. You don't need to know what your passion is to make a commitment. Starting is as simple as picking what feels right to you and just doing it. If it's not your passion, you will know it. In that case, pick another one and just start again. Don't be afraid to change your mind.

You Do Have Passion

Many people believe they don't have a passion and therefore they need to find one. But how do you find something that isn't missing in the first place? It's like trying to find your glasses when you are wearing them. Your glasses aren't missing. All you have to do is to acknowledge that they are there. Everyone has passion. You are just unaware you have it.

> *It's not that you don't know what your passion is.*
> *It's just that you forget it along the way.*

As children grow up and learn to be adults, they lose part of themselves trying to fit in with others. They become so in tune with what society wants them to be that they become out of tune with what they love.

Just because you don't remember the last time you did something you love doesn't mean that you don't have a passion. Sometimes, you aren't aware you love doing something, even though you are doing it because it feels so natural to you. Becoming conscious of what you love to do will take time for some people. But don't be discouraged. Start anyway, because taking action might just trigger your lost memory.

A Chicken-and-Egg Situation

There are two different views online: Some believe that you need to figure out your passion first and take action later. Others, like Cal Newport (author of *So Good They Can't Ignore You*), argue that you need to put in effort first, be good at it, and then you will develop a passion for it.

My question on this debate is: Does it even matter?

Is it important to know whether your passion comes before taking action or after taking action? It's the same as asking the question: What came first, the chicken or the egg? It is pointless.

> *Both the chicken and the egg are yummy.*
> *Who cares which came first?*

It doesn't matter if you think that you are born with a pre-existing passion or not. It doesn't matter if you discover your passion only much later. As I mentioned in chapter 1, **both passion and action are important.**

The advice "follow your passion" doesn't tell you when you should have your passion figured out. It doesn't tell you to find your passion first. All it says is that when you discover what your passion is, follow it.

Myth #2: I Need to Have Talent to Do What I Love

It's easy to mix up the two: what you are good at (your strengths) and what you love to do (your passion). People tend to love the things they do well because it boosts their self-esteem. But you don't need to be good at something to enjoy doing it. You can have fun doing things you are not good at.

Write Music when You Can't Hear Music

One day, as I'm waiting for the train with my friend, she asked me, "You know, I always loved music, but I never thought of writing any songs. How do you come out with the melody? How do you get started?"

"I usually play on my keyboard and start singing any melody that comes to my mind," I replied.

"That simple?" she doubted.

"Yup. In fact, you don't even need to know any musical instrument to write songs. My first song is composed with a tape recorder. I just sing into my tape recorder and listen to it repeatedly to write the lyrics," I explained.

***

Most people have the perception that you need to be born with some mad, crazy talent before you can pursue your passion. This is far from the truth. I can't hear music notes well. I find it difficult to discern if a note is higher or lower in pitch. But that doesn't stop me from writing songs. I still write songs. It just takes me a longer time to find the notes to my melody on the keyboard.

> *Don't let what talents you think you should have*
> *stop you from doing what you love.*

What you think you need to get started might not always be what you really need to get started. Beethoven still continued to compose his symphonies in spite of going deaf. When you love to do something, you will find ways to make it work.

Talent Is So Overrated

Talent is just a head start. It will only get you so far. A pianist who is musically talented but doesn't invest the time to practice won't get better at it.

People who are passionate naturally want to learn and get better at what they do. They will put in the time and effort to develop their playing skills. Eventually, they will be familiar with the score and their fingers will become stronger. It is just a matter of time before they catch up and surpass the people who have talent but do not practice.

Talented people's accomplishments
seem deceptively effortless.

When you see talented people on TV, you don't see the amount of work they put in to master their craft. People tend to attribute the celebrity's success to his or her innate talent because the performance seems so effortless. It's easy to forget what the performers do off-screen daily to get to where they are.

Opera singers practice for countless hours to reach and stabilize their high notes. Athletes run many times a day to improve their timing. Actors have to reshoot their scenes repeatedly to get the best takes for the audiences. What we see on screen is just the final product of their hard work.

All these talented people have to spend many hours practicing, too. Without passion in what they do, it takes more effort to do the same thing over and over again.

Myth #3: Pursuing Passion Makes Me Selfish

Recently, I was shocked to hear about some clients of a friend who divorced because the spouse decided to pursue his passion as a career.

I understand passionate people can sometimes be perceived as selfish. They tend to spend more time on what they love and less time with their partners, family, and friends. And giving up a higher-paying job for passion might bring in less money for the family. But still, divorce feels extreme to me.

No One Has to Be Worse Off

How someone pursues his passion depends on the individual. You don't have to impact the people around you. If you are passionate about your family, you will find time for them. You will continue to provide for them.

Before I left my job as an accountant, I made it clear to my parents that they would still receive the same monthly allowance that I was giving them at the time. I wasn't going to shortchange them for my passion.

Just because you are pursuing your passion, you don't have to give up other areas of your life. You don't have to sacrifice one for the other. Chapter 8 discusses how to handle your multiple passions.

Leaving the Job You Hate Is the Least Selfish Thing You Can Do

One time, I was browsing the Internet and someone's comment perplexed me. It went something like this: "If everyone is doing what they love, who is going to do the jobs that no one loves? Am I being selfish for chasing my dreams?"

It was as though the person were asking: "If everyone is happy, who is going to be miserable?"

I don't get it.

Is he saying that there must be someone out there miserable in order for others to be happy?

Or, is he saying if everyone else is miserable, he will feel guilty to be happy?

Or, does he think he's being selfless for doing a job he hates as others get to pursue their dreams?

***

I've another view when it comes to leaving the job you hate.

First, something that you don't love to do doesn't mean that someone else wouldn't love it. Sweeping the floor might be boring to you, but others might enjoy cleaning up the environment. I have seen tree cutters who are happy and having fun with what they do. It looks tough working outdoors, but they enjoy it. Plus, everyone has different goals in life. Not everyone will pursue their passion as a career. And not everyone wants to.

Second, the industry will find a way out. If there's a lack of people in an industry, the market will correct itself and attract employees by increasing salaries. If not, companies will have to address their inefficiency by redesigning their work processes or automating their systems. The improvements they make actually will help the companies and the employees in the long run.

Removing yourself from a job you don't like is actually good for the company's morale. Not only do you do yourself a big favor, you also give the company a chance to hire somebody who will be passionate at the job. Happy employees breed a better working culture. Having an unmotivated employee, on the other hand, slows down the company's efficiency and brings morale down.

Loving Yourself Is Not a Selfish Act

As I mention in chapter 1, doing what you love is a way of loving yourself. There's nothing selfish about that. In fact, it's essential and healthy to love yourself first before extending your love to others. When you are positive and happy, you can influence the people around you to be the same.

When you put other people's needs over your own, it makes you feel neglected and unimportant. If you don't take care of your needs, who else is going to do it for you? And if you can't even take care of your own needs, how are you going to take care of other people's needs?

Myth #4: It's Too Late for Me to Do What I Love

Last year, I received a call from an insurance telemarketer. She was surprised that I was switching careers.

She commented: "I also love animation, but I'm not like you. You're young. You can pursue what you want. I'm too old to do what I love."

That set me thinking about age. Are we ever too old to do what we love?

I understand that she is probably more than forty years old and has a family to support. And if she changes her career now, she has at most twenty years in her new career before she retires. But what bothers me is when people use their age to justify their decisions.

Age is a convenient excuse

The issue here isn't about age. You can still make a career change and achieve great success regardless of your age. Look at these famous examples below:

- **Tom Clancy:** He spent fifteen years in the insurance industry before he published his first novel, *The Hunt for Red October,* in his mid thirties.
- **Julia Child:** She started learning how to cook in her late thirties and had her first cooking show, *The French Chef,* when she reached the age of fifty-one.
- **Colonel Sanders:** He franchised KFC (Kentucky Fried Chicken) at the age of sixty-two after being a fireman and an insurance salesman.
- **Grandma Moses:** She started painting in her late seventies and her paintings were then used in holiday cards.
- **Fauja Singh:** He reignited his passion for running and ran his first marathon at the age of eighty-nine.

Age is just too convenient an excuse for inaction. Many times, it's actually your fear that holds you back, not your age. In fact, people in their twenties also think it is too late for them. They feel they have already spent a lot of time in their current careers and on their education. Starting all over again feels too risky. What if their new careers don't suit them?

Fear of change is universal across all ages.

Some Passions Are Meant to Be Pursued Later

Passion comes to you at different points in your life. Some passions take time to emerge. I only become aware that animation was an occupation in my late twenties although animation studios have been around in Singapore for quite some time. Just because my passion in animation came later doesn't mean that it's too late for me to pursue it. It just means that I am meant to pursue it at a later stage of my life.

Even if you are older and you feel that you can't do those vigorous activities that you love anymore—such as martial arts, hip hop dancing, or soccer—there is always something for all ages. You can do yoga, ballroom dancing, or golf instead. Doing what you love is not a privilege for the young. You can always start something new.

If You Miss the Boat, Take another Boat

Imagine you are a new explorer. You arrive on an island in a boat. On the dock, there's a sign that reads: "The boat comes and departs once every year. Decide if you want to board the boat now or stay on the island."

You decide to explore the island for a year. But after a while, you feel unhappy living on the island: it is boring; it does not fit your personality; it's meaningless to stay on. So you try to swim away a couple of times, but you fail. So, you decide to wait for the next boat.

Over the year, you get used to the island. You know where the food and water are. You have built a nice house for yourself. Life is stable. When the boat comes back one year later, you hesitate.

"What if the other islands are worse than this island? What if there is no such comfort on another island? I will lose everything I have here now and I will have to start all over again."

You walk up and down the dock. You can't decide whether to take the boat or not. Finally, the boat leaves and guess what? You're not on it and you have to stay.

Each year you wait for the boat to arrive, only to see it depart without you. Although you dislike the island, you have settled down. Eventually, you forget about this boat that can take you to other islands...

***

This is what it's like when you stay in a job you dislike for many years. It's not that it's too late to do what you love— you just become too comfortable with what you don't love doing. If you had left the island the first year, you could have enjoyed your remaining years doing what you love.

But even if you have missed the boat for the last ten years, you can still take the boat right now and find an island that you love. There is always another boat for you to take. It's never too late.

Myth #5: I'm Too Busy to Do What I Love

In September 2013, I made a tough decision. I decided to resign from my accounting job earlier than planned. My original plan seemed perfect. Complete my animation studies, find another job, and then resign. It was flawless other than the fact I wasn't able to execute it.

Halfway through my course, I found it difficult to juggle my work and studies. I must say I'm quite a badass when it comes to pursuing my passion. I spent all my nights after work doing my animation assignment and attending lessons. I didn't go out on weekends unless it was absolutely necessary. Most of my free time was dedicated to my animation assignments.

Even then, I felt that I did not have enough time to do what I love. I didn't want to submit crappy work to my mentor. I knew that I could do much better work than what I was doing. I told myself I needed to find time for my passion, for example:

- I would wake up at 6 a.m. to do my assignment before going to work.
- I would do my assignment till 2 a.m. and still go to work the next day.
- I tried to do things faster at work so that I could come back home earlier to do my animation.
- I sacrificed some of my routines, such as watching TV programs, listening to music, and exercising.
- I gave up on my time to write songs and attend music lessons.

It didn't take me long to realize that this routine wasn't working. My eyes started to give me problems; they were in pain and crying for help. I'd been sitting in front of the computer seven days a week for the whole day. It was really bad for my eyes.

That was when I decided to throw my plan out the window. I *had* to quit!

You Have to Make Time for Your Passion

There is no way you can have more time for your passion unless you make time for it. The concept of time is based on priorities. Everyone has twenty-four hours a day. Whether you have the time to do something or not really depends on how you choose to spend your time. If doing something you love is important to you, you will find time for it.

> *Having no time for passion*
> *is like having no time to brush your teeth.*

If you have the time to brush your teeth, wash your hair, and sleep, you will have time for passion. They all serve the same purpose: You brush your teeth to keep your mouth and teeth clean. You wash your hair so that it smells nice. You sleep to replenish your energy. All these are acts of loving yourself. So is doing what you love; it is just in another form.

In addition to loving your body, you should love yourself spiritually, too. If you can develop the habit of brushing your teeth, you can definitely add passion as one of the habits of your daily routine.

Where Does All My Time Go?

Most people are too busy to do what they love because they are unconscious of how they spend their time.

Don't think that when you love something,
you will remember to do it.

There are little distractions everywhere that waste your time. TV, cell phones, the Internet, and social media are all potential time wasters.

Every time I catch myself doing mindless stuff like surfing the web aimlessly, I feel like I've been knocked out and brought to a new location. I forget what my initial purpose was and have no idea why I went to the website in the first place.

Unnecessary tasks also waste a lot of your time. Do you really have to attend so many meetings at work? Do you really need to complete all your work by today? Do you really have to watch so many TV series? Do you really have to spend so much time on making everything perfect?

Check and see if all your tasks are essential. Eliminate them if they are not because being too busy is not good for you. You are not leaving any room for unexpected opportunities. And you are not taking the time to enjoy the journey.

Myth #6: Doing Too Much of What You Love Kills the Passion

Some people think that if you turn your passion into a career and do too much of it, you are going to end up hating it. It is true that doing anything excessively (regardless of whether you love it or not) for long hours will create burnout. However, it is not doing too much that is bad. What's bad is not taking enough breaks to rest.

Even Passion Needs to Sleep

The first time I went to New York, I was super excited to watch the Broadway musicals. Before the trip, I watched tons of clips online. I planned out all the shows I wanted to see. I just felt so ready to watch them all!

On our first night in New York, my friends and I rushed to catch the musical *Chicago*. We bought the tickets, had our quick dinner, and eagerly waited for our first musical in New York to begin.

But as I was watching *Chicago* in the theater, something strange happened to me. I felt my eyes closing. My eyelids were heavy. I tried to pull them open, but I couldn't. The theater was so dark and comfortable.... The actors and actresses were chattering on stage.... We were sitting right at the back of the theater.... Then I fell asleep.

Suddenly, the orchestra struck and it woke me up. I leaned forward to watch the performance and pulled my eyes as wide open as possible. Before I knew it, I fell asleep again.

I slept in the city that never sleeps.

During the whole musical, I just drifted in and out of the show in a trance. And unfortunately, I missed three-quarters of the show. I wanted to enjoy the show badly, but I just could not keep myself awake. It was my first time taking a long-distance flight. It took about one day to fly from Singapore to New York. And I had never experienced jet lag before.

After that day, I concluded that passion cannot win over jet lag.

No matter how passionate you are, passion can only provide you with so much spiritual energy. You still need to have the physical energy to carry out what you love to do. If you are tired physically, you will not be able to enjoy your passion. Always take a rest when necessary.

There's No Need to Conserve Passion

Passion is not a candle. With a candle, the more you use it, the less it becomes, and someday it will disappear. The opposite is true of passion. The more time you spend on your passion, the more you enjoy it and the more energized you become. If you get tired of your passion easily, it's probably not your real passion, or you don't take enough breaks.

Use as much "passion energy" as possible. There is no need to conserve your passion for the future. Doing less of what you love now doesn't mean that your passion will last longer; it just means that you are not using your passion to its fullest potential. You are not getting all the benefits that passion can give you.

Don't Be Afraid to Lose Your Passion

Some people who discover their passion are very afraid of losing it. They think that their passion can be taken away from them. The truth is once you love something, you will love it for life. You can never lose it.

Passions do, however, evolve over time. When one passion subsides, it's making way for a new one to emerge. It doesn't mean that your previous passion has died. It's just time to explore other passions.

The energy level for each passion varies throughout your lifetime. It doesn't stay static. When I was in my teens, I loved to write songs. But back then, I took a two-year break from songwriting to focus on my 'A' Levels. After the two years, I picked up music again and started learning a keyboard and singing in music schools. Not only had my passion for songwriting not died, my songwriting skills actually improved.

Now, I'm taking another break from songwriting because my passion in animation and writing are stronger. I still love songwriting. But I'm just making time for my other passions.

> *Fear prevents you from taking action and that in itself is already killing your passion.*

Don't let your fear of losing your passion stop you from doing more of what you love. Just let your passion grow naturally.

Myth #7: Do What You Love and the Money Will Follow

Making money from your passion is great. You get to satisfy both your financial and spiritual needs, but **not all passion pays you.** Here are some scenarios when passion doesn't pay you:

- You have no idea how to monetize your passion.
- You have not acquired the necessary skills to make money out of your passion.

- You love what you do but you don't love making money from it.
- You treat passion as a hobby. You have no plans to improve your skills.
- Your passion doesn't provide value to others or satisfy their needs.

Some entrepreneurs see doing what they love as a tool to making lots of money. The issue with that focus is that to increase your income, you have to perform money-making activities, such as marketing and selling, which might not be your passion.

Money Needs to Be Earned; It Doesn't Follow

A person who loves what he does but doesn't make any effort to market himself won't make any money. Let's say a person loves to paint. If he just paints all day at home but no one knows about it, no one will buy his paintings. No matter how good his paintings are or how much he loves painting, he will not earn any money.

As I mention previously in the opening story, Simon is successful because he pays attention to marketing. If he didn't take the time to market himself and his work, he won't have received the recognition he receive today.

Whether to make money from your passion or not is your choice. If your definition of success is to make the most money you can, pursuing your passion might not be the fastest or best way to do so. But if you choose to earn money from your passion, it will be helpful to pick up other skills such as sales and marketing, and your passion can help you acquire those skills. I'll share more about this in chapter 9.

You Are Not the Star

When it comes to making money, it's never about you or what you love to do. You are not the star. The focus is on the person who is potentially paying you—your customer. He is paying you money to satisfy his needs and solve his problems.

> *Why should your customer even care*
> *about your passion?*

To make money from what you love to do, you need to figure out how to provide values with your passion.

- In business, you need to create products and services that are of value to your customers.
- As an employee, you need to deliver what is expected of you and beyond.
- As a jobseeker, you need to have the relevant skills and experience. The cost to hire you must be justified before a company will hire you.

Passion alone is not enough. It doesn't get you a job or a client. Remember, you only play a supporting role in this money-making drama. Your job is to support the star. Give him the support he needs to play his role and you'll get paid.

Myth #8: Pursuing My Passion Will Make Me Poor

I invest lots of money in education because I love to learn. But pursuing a passion doesn't have to be costly; it can be cheap or even free. Nowadays, you can **learn almost anything online for free.**

- Don't know how to start a blog? Just search on YouTube for a demonstration.
- Not sure what to major in? Try a module for free online at Coursera. There are a wide selection of MOOCs (massive open online courses) created by universities around the world.
- Never used Photoshop before? Google it and find out how to create a nice wallpaper for your desktop.

Aside from online resources, you can borrow books from the library, sign up for classes in your community, and volunteer your time with companies. Start using free or cheaper resources first. Then, decide whether to invest more in paid programs to further your knowledge.

No Need to Quit Your Current Job

You don't have to commit all your time and sacrifice all your income to pursue your passion. You can pursue your passion as a hobby and start small first. Then, slowly integrate more passion into your life. For example:

- Develop your skills until you have developed them enough to get a job.
- Build your business on the side.
- Ask your boss for more flexible hours.
- Switch to part-time jobs with less office hours.

It takes some trial and error plus some adjustments to get the right balance between income and passion. But there is no need to be poor and choose between the two.

Passion Is Not Charity

Passion is something that you love doing and don't mind doing for free. But that doesn't imply you should treat your passion as charity and do work for free. You deserve to earn income from your passions.

Many people believe their passions will not make them much money. That's because they haven't figured out a way to monetize them. Following what others have already done successfully gives you some ideas how to start. But it's also normal to start without knowing exactly how to monetize your passion.

Take Mark Zuckerberg, cofounder of Facebook, for example. When he first started Facebook, he was not thinking how he would profit from it. He probably wasn't anticipating that Facebook would make billions and get listed on the NASDAQ stock exchange. He simply started with a mission to make the world open and tested his ideas on college students first.

You will figure out how to monetize your passion when you take action and test your ideas out. What works for someone else might or might not work for you.

Finding a job and starting a business are not the only ways to make money. There are other ways to monetize your passion if you do some research and leverage on the platforms available. For example:

- Create your own products (e.g., write a book and self-publish with Amazon's CreateSpace).
- Provide services on your website or through online platforms (e.g., bid on and complete programming or web design projects at Freelancer.com).
- Sell affiliates products and advertisement on your website (e.g., find affiliates' products from like Clickbank.com and advertisements using Google AdSense).
- Earn royalties from your design and photos through online retailers (e.g., upload your design and create your own merchandise on Zazzle.com).
- Source for funds before you even start your project (e.g., create a project on crowd-funding platforms like Kickstarter.com and ask people to donate money).

The possibilities are endless now with the help of technology. Just use a little creativity and pick the methods that best suit you!

PART 2:
UNDERSTANDING FEAR

Chapter 3

WHAT IS STOPPING YOU FROM REALIZING YOUR DREAMS?

LARRY JACOBSON TRADED EVERYTHING HE HAD to realize his boyhood dream of sailing around the world. Not only did he give up a good income, his long-term relationship, and security, he had to let go of his career identity as a successful entrepreneur— something he had spent twenty years building.

Larry's dream was first conceived when he was thirteen years old. He had broken his leg and was stuck in bed in a hip-to-toe cast for more than three months. To cheer him up, his mother brought home magazines for him to read. He became interested in the ones on boats. Being bedridden, he would look out of his window and imagine sailing to faraway places on a boat.

And that ignited his dream of sailing around the world.

After the cast came off, Larry was ready to "cast off" and seized every opportunity to sail. For example:

- At thirteen, he taught himself sailing with an eight-foot Styrofoam Sea Snark dinghy brought home by his brother from the trash bin.
- At sixteen, he saved $900 from odd jobs and bought a fourteen-foot Hobie Cat.
- After school each day, he would ride six miles on his bicycle to Alamitos Bay and practiced sailing.
- In university, he joined the sailing team.
- After graduation, he signed on as a sailboat crew member to sail across the Pacific Ocean.

However, pursuing a dream as big as Larry's took both a great deal of time and money. Circumnavigating the globe would take him a few years, and he didn't have the money to do so. To finance his dream, he created a company that sold group-incentive travel programs to corporations.

The company was doing well at first. But then the Gulf War started and took away most of his international business. That didn't stop Larry from still pursuing his dream. The war could take away his business, but it could not take away his passion.

It didn't matter how long it took or what obstacles he had, he knew he would achieve his dream one day. So, he kept moving forward. In 1991, he devised a plan and wrote down his ultimate goal on a piece of paper: *"Own a 50-foot boat and begin my journey around the world ten years from now."*

Fear of Letting Go of His Identity

Fast forward to 2001. By this time, Larry had held onto his dream for thirty-three years. Finally, the day came when it was time for Larry to act on his dream. Yet, he felt torn.

"The good things you have in your life are the biggest obstacle to achieving your grandest dreams."

To pursue his dream, Larry had to let go of all the good things in his life:

- **Income:** He went from earning a solid income to earning absolutely nothing.
- **His twenty-year relationship with his partner:** His partner was not interested in going sailing with him, so Larry made the tough decision to go without him.
- **Security:** Larry said farewell to all the familiar things, people, and routines in his life that kept him secure, including his beautiful house in the Berkeley Hills.
- **Career:** He left behind his successful travel business, which was highly regarded in the industry.

Even though he built his business with his dream in mind, giving it up was tough. It represented twenty years of hard work. How could he walk away just like that?

More importantly, what would his next identity be? A sailor, an explorer, or perhaps simply an impulsive adventurer? Selling his business also meant saying good-bye to his identity, and this was scary for him. He was in uncharted waters. All he had as a guide was his heart and his vision.

But at the same time, Larry felt liberated once he had made the decision to start over. Sailing gave him freedom. He had the ability to choose where to anchor and where to go next. He had a clear vision for success, too. Whenever he closed his eyes in his office, he could see himself successfully completing his journey, sailing under the Golden Gate Bridge, looking up to see his friends and family cheering for him upon his return.

He was so drawn to his vision that he had to do it!

So later that year, Larry set sail under the Golden Gate Bridge with two other friends—just as he had pictured years before. He completed his adventure six years later with a whole new lifetime of experiences and lessons learned.

Above all, he found a new identity for himself while sailing across the ocean. He became the author of his memoir, *The Boy Behind the Gate,* and a motivational speaker to encourage others to follow their dreams.

Key Lessons from Larry's Story

1. Only you can make your dreams come true.

Not many people would want to sail around the world like Larry. In fact, his family thought he was crazy because they didn't share the same passion and vision that he had.

Larry had to spend many years in business to earn enough to fulfill his dream. No one else was going to give him the money to do that. It was his dream, not theirs.

**"Who are you expecting to make
your dreams come true for you?"**

Everyone has unique dreams and it is up to the individual to realize them. Don't wait for others to support or help you in your quest. If you want your dream to come true, you need to take action and make it happen.

2. Pursuing one passion often leads to another.

Two years into his adventure around the world, Larry discovered his passion for writing. It came about when he wanted to record and share important events from his journey with his friends and family.

When he returned to California, he had more than two thousand pages of journals and e-mails written from his trip. He spent the next three years writing and organizing the resources for his book. He also became a motivational speaker to inspire others to pursue their dreams.

Larry never knew he had the desire to write until he set sail. He wouldn't have found his passion for writing and speaking if he hadn't let go of his old identity and explored his passion as he had envisioned.

3. Fears of the future are mostly unjustified.

It seemed risky for Larry to give up everything to pursue his dream. What would he do when he came back? Where would he live? There was no way for him to know until he let go.

Most fears are exaggerated. They appear when you imagine the situation to be bigger and scarier than it is. But what you imagine is not the truth!

Larry still made a living and had a roof over his head after his trip. He became happier and richer in terms of experience. The material wealth he thought he needed for survival and to be happy turned out to be unimportant to him.

People are often afraid to pursue what they love because they only see what they lose in the process. What they fail to realize are the gains they can receive from following their passion.

Don't Let Fears Stop You

As I explained at the beginning of the book, taking action is vital in pursuing your passion. However, fear often blocks you from taking any action. It creates resistance and disrupts the flow and energy that passion naturally has. It slows you down. It makes you worry.

Fear also suppresses your creativity. It stops you from generating creative ideas to pursue your passion. When you are afraid you can't make a living from your passion, you believe it to be true and accept things as they are. You won't think of ways to monetize your passion.

In this and the following three chapters, I will discuss some of the common fears you often face in pursuing a passion and suggest ways that you can unblock them.

You Frankenstein Your Fears

If fear hinders action, all you need to do is to find the source, remove it, and you can pursue your dreams freely, right? Simple, isn't it? Well, I have news for you. The creator of your fear is you. You create your own Frankenstein monster.

It doesn't matter if you are afraid of spiders, heights, or dogs. Fear is a self-made product. You cannot blame dogs for creating your fear because not everyone is afraid of dogs. Some people love their pet dogs dearly. So, why do dogs scare you and not others? To different people, the same thing or event means different things. The thing itself does not create fear or make you afraid. It is what you imagine will happen (for example, the dog is going to bite me) that makes you afraid and creates fear.

So, the one who is really stopping you from pursuing your dreams is **none other than you!** You are responsible for both your dreams and fears.

Don't Scare Yourself before the Monster Appears

Do you know what the scariest part of a horror movie is? It's not when the monster appears or when the murderer appears with a knife from behind. The scariest part is before the monster or the murderer appears. It is your constant anticipation of danger that scares you.

It is the same when it comes to pursuing your passion. Pursuing your passion is supposed to be fun and there is nothing scary about it. It is all the negative things you anticipate will happen that makes it scary.

Every time you experience fear, keep your cool first. Don't run away when you have not even seen the monster yet. For all you know, the monster might not be as scary as you imagine it to be. Sometimes, the monster doesn't even appear in the scene you anticipate it to appear in.

Why Do You Have to Uncover Your Fears?

Not identifying your fears doesn't mean that they are not there. It's like tripping over an obstacle again and again without knowing that there's an obstacle in front of you. It's like having an anchor that pulls you down and stops you from moving forward without you knowing there's even an anchor there. Uncovering your fears helps you to steer away from these obstacles and free those anchors.

Kids Are Afraid of the Dark; So Are Adults

Kids are afraid of the dark because they imagine scary monsters lurking in the dark. Adults are the same way, too. We get scared when we cannot see our future and imagine the worst thing that can happen.

> *To see what's hiding in the dark,*
> *simply switch on your lights.*

When you shine a light on your fears, you are more aware of them. When you can see them better, you question if there's a need to be afraid. However, if you brush your fears aside and not examine them, you are just going to believe that your fears are true. You are just going to assume that there are monsters lurking in the dark when it's only your imagination.

Fears Are Very Good at Hiding

Sometimes, you have fears that you don't even know you have. They cover themselves easily with your other beliefs, and your behaviors are controlled by them automatically without you even noticing.

For example, people believe they are lazy because they procrastinate often. But the reality is people procrastinate not because they are lazy. They procrastinate because they are afraid:

- **Fear of failure:** What if I start this project and it doesn't work out?
- **Fear of making mistakes:** What if I pick the wrong project?
- **Fear of commitment:** What if I commit to do this project and have no other time for other things I love?
- **Fear of changes:** I have not done a similar project like this before. What if this is too challenging for me?
- **Fear of success:** What if I successfully complete this project and others expect me to be successful all the time?

It's easy to label yourself as "lazy" because then it's part of your personality and there's nothing you can do about it. But the label "lazy" is only an excuse to cover up your fear. Forcing yourself to work harder doesn't help, because the root of your problem isn't that you are lazy; the root of your problem is that you have fears you don't wish to touch.

Being aware of your fear is already one big step toward being fearless.

Identifying your fears helps you to get down to the core of your inaction. It tells you why you react certain ways to certain events and uncovers the beliefs you aren't unaware of. Fear is afraid to get caught. He knows that once he is caught, he becomes weaker and loses much of his power over you.

In chapters 4 and 5, you will find more examples and stories on fears. They will increase your awareness about the fears you have.

What Exactly Is "Fearless Passion"?

"Fearless Passion" doesn't mean that you have zero fear when it comes to pursuing your passion. **To be "fearless" means you just "fear less."**

It means you are at peace with your fears and they don't stop you from taking actions. My intention in this book is to get you to the point where you start to take action on your passion.

You start to become fearless
when you take action.

The focus is not on fear. The focus is having the courage to take action. I'm not going to teach you how to eliminate, conquer, triumph, or fight your fears. Instead, I'm going to share how you can get the most out of your fears and use them to your advantage in chapter 6.

You Aren't Alone in the Fear Industry

It is normal to have fears. Everyone has them. Your peers, your parents, even successful people have fears, too. You're not alone. You are not any worse off for being afraid.

What's important, though, is to not let fear stop you from taking action and guide you away from the things you love to do.

Fear Is Really Not the Problem

When it comes to pursuing your passion, you have two choices:

1. Be fearful and not do anything about it; or
2. Be fearful but take action on your passion.

Whichever option you choose, you have to be 100 percent responsible for how you react to your fears. Never use your fear as an excuse for inaction. Don't blame the economy for not doing well, your family for not supporting you, or yourself for not being good enough to get what you want in life. Every time you blame something or someone else, you are giving your power away and shirking from your responsibility.

Remember, you have a choice—accept your responsibilities!

Dreams Create Reality

Dreams are important. What most people don't realize, though is that all things are created by dreams. **The dream has to come first before the reality can occur.** Dreams create reality.

To make anything possible, you must first have a vision of what it looks like. Someone must have first dreamt about it before they created something.

Neil Armstrong didn't step onto the moon because other people before him had done it and proved that it was possible. It came from a dream that President John F. Kennedy had. Every invention around us—such as the laptop, computer, Smartphone, TV, DVD, Internet, and so on—comes from someone's dream of having it.

Just because no one has done it before doesn't mean that it's not possible. If everybody had been fearful of realizing their dreams and didn't strive for the impossible, then there wouldn't be any inventions today.

Dreaming Needs a Regular Workout

Dreaming is like a muscle. If you don't use it often, you will need some exercises to get your dream back in shape again. But dreaming is free and fun. You don't need to spend any money or resource to dream. It doesn't take a long time to conjure up a dream. You can dream as big as you want!

It doesn't matter if you think it is a good idea or not, realistic or unrealistic, achievable or unachievable, possible or impossible. When it comes to dreaming, anything is possible if you believe it so. **The Universe doesn't discriminate against any dream.**

Don't worry if your dream is possible or not. Don't worry about how you are going to do it. Don't limit your dream because you are afraid you cannot obtain it.

Shut down your critical mind and let your inner child take over for a moment. Just have fun with dreaming and capture your dreams on paper. The reason for doing this is because you don't want to filter your dreams but instead to develop a habit for dreaming and strengthen that dreaming muscle. The more you dream, the better you get at it.

Why Don't Your Dreams Come True?

1. **You don't genuinely want it in the first place.** It is somebody else's dream or something you think you need. When your dream does not reflect what your heart truly

desires, it won't come true.

2. **You don't genuinely believe it will come true.** Several things happen when you don't believe in your dreams: First, you don't act upon them. Second, you give up on them easily. If you genuinely believe your dreams will come true, you will take action because you know that your action will pay off one day.

3. **You want it too badly now.** Wanting it more does not make you any closer to your dreams. Taking action does. Wanting your dreams to come true immediately shows a lack of trust in the Universe, a lack of belief in yourself, and a lack of belief that it will come true.

4. **Trying to control how you achieve your dreams.** Again, this is a lack of faith in the Universe. When you try to control all the steps to achieve your dreams, you miss signs given to you by the Universe. These signs are like express passes to your dreams.

5. **Your fears sabotage you.** Sometimes, when you are close to achieving your dreams, you self-sabotage with your fears and beliefs. For dreams to come true, actions have to be taken. When opportunities that you wish for present themselves to you, you must have the courage to take advantage of them.

Dreams are possible. But as adults, we are caught up with reality so much that we lose our ability to dream. Right from the beginning, we decide what is possible or not possible, even before we have a chance to act on it.

> If you don't try it out, how can you conclude that something is impossible or does not work?

Chapter 4

THE GREATEST FEAR: NOT HAVING ENOUGH MONEY

"HOW DO YOU FIND THE COURAGE to pursue your passion?" You probably wouldn't be reading this right now if my friend had not asked me this question.

In December 2012, I attended my college classmate's wedding. That day, I told my friends that I would soon be leaving my accounting job to concentrate on my animation studies. That raised quite a number of eyebrows. In particular, they were concerned about the impact it would have on my finances.

Being an accountant is a very stable job. Every company needs accountants. Without a doubt, there are fewer animation jobs in the market, and it is much harder to find a good one. Switching to a new career also meant I had to restart and take a substantial pay cut.

Plus, leaving a job without another job is crazy!

How would I support myself?

What really stood out from our conversation was when one of my friends, Cleo, asked me how I found the courage to chase my passion.

Cleo is passionate about making brides look pretty. She had been doing bridal makeup outside her job for almost five years. In terms of experience in pursuing passion as a career, she was way ahead of me. She already had a word-of-mouth advantage in her industry. Yet, she told me she didn't have the courage to do what she loves full-time. She was afraid she couldn't support herself.

I didn't answer her question as fully as I would have wanted to that day. Probably I didn't have the answer back then, anyway. But it did get me thinking how our fear of not having enough money could hold us back from pursuing our passion. Her question inspired me to write this chapter.

At this point in writing, I'm happy to say Cleo now does her bridal makeup business full-time. Although she left her job because her company closed down, she now knows that she can survive working full-time at her passion.

I'm Not as Courageous as You Think

This is the second time I have returned to HBO Asia to do part-time work after I resigned. And I really hate myself for doing so.

It's not because I have to wake up earlier.
It's not because I dislike working there.
It's not even because I hate accounting.
It's because I have chosen money over passion.

Accounting does pay me better than animation. In fact, animation pays me absolutely nothing right now. But it's not fair to conclude that I can't earn as much in animation as I do in accounting because I'm relatively new to animation and haven't spent as much time in this field as I have in accounting. Of course, it's not going to pay as well right now.

Each time I went back to work part-time, I regretted it. I felt like quitting. It stole precious time away from my passions. Sometimes, I came back from work feeling too tired and de-energized to focus on my passions. Why did I put myself back into this situation again? Why was I here again?

It's tormenting!

The first time I went back, I thought my main motivation was to help my ex-colleagues because of a manpower shortage. Money was secondary. This time, however, I knew that I had been lying to myself about the last time I had returned there.

I came back because I was afraid that I wouldn't have enough money to support myself. I'm afraid I won't have enough money to attend my animation graduation in California. I wanted to make some money to feel secure again. I enjoy helping out my friends, too, but now I realize my action was mostly motivated by fear. It was almost creepy that *every time I feel financially insecure, I'll get a call from my boss to come back and work.*

And every time I accepted it on the spot.

I'm just an average person like you. I'm not as courageous as Cleo thought I was. I'm afraid, too, and it took me two part-time work intervals to realize that.

Key Lessons from These Two Stories

1. Most fears are universal.

Cleo thought I was more courageous than she was. It turned out that I was just as afraid as she was. Everyone has fears and most of them are common. I wouldn't be writing about all these fears in my book if I didn't personally experience them.

Most people assume others have more courage and conclude that's why they are able to do what they love. It's not true. People pursue their passion because they decide to do so. It's not because they have no fears or less fears. They just don't let their fears run their life. They decide what is best for their life.

2. Fear can make your passion stronger.

It is okay to be afraid when pursuing your passion. You learn along the way. Although I went back to my old job twice, at least I recognized how strong my passion was.

The first time around when I was still studying animation, doing the other job solidified my passion for animation. I realized how much I loved animation and how unwilling I was to trade my time for money. This time at the old job has strengthened my passion in writing this book. I became more aware of my fear. And ironically, my fear becomes a story for this book.

I was uncertain how strong my passions were until my fear led me away from them. I was not sure how badly I wanted to write this book and how much I love to animate until I went back to accounting.

> **3. Making more money might not make you happier.**
>
> Look at me. I'm not earning any income since leaving my job. Realistically, I should be happier to work part-time and make extra cash. But I'm not.
>
> Going back to work creates a fierce tug-of-war between my mind and my heart. And it really makes me unhappy. My mind thinks it's smart to earn more money and save up for the future. My heart, on the other hand, feels miserable because it's not allowed to do what it loves.
>
> All I want is to have my mind and heart working harmoniously together. I didn't anticipate that making more money would create so much chaos.

Money Can't Buy You Happiness

Have you ever thought why you want to earn so much money in the first place?

- Is it the house you want to buy?
- Is it the country you want to visit?
- Or is it the comfort you want to enjoy?

Whatever the reason, money is just a medium to exchange what you want for it. It is a by-product. It is actually the house, the experience, or the comfort that you can buy with money that makes you happy, not money itself.

Money definitely can both allow you to buy necessities and also enhance your life. But you will reach a point where having more money doesn't equate to more happiness.

Are You Gambling for Happiness?

Some of you might want to earn as much money as you can now, so that you can retire and enjoy that life earlier. The question is if you're going to do what you love upon retirement anyway, why not do it now?

Why postpone your happiness?

Moreover, you can't be certain how much money you need to make in order to retire happily. If there isn't any certainty in the outcome, then aren't you gambling?

People think I'm a risk taker because I had the courage to quit my job and pursue my passion. I see myself as risk adverse. *I'm cashing in my happiness today by doing what I love because I know for certain it'll make me happy.*

I don't know what will happen tomorrow. I don't want to do things that I hate and wait till I have a large sum of money before I enjoy my life.

Don't compromise your happiness now to make more money because wanting to be happy in the future is like gambling for happiness.

Do what you love as you make money.

Money Can't Provide You with Financial Security

Financial security is relative and vague. Like happiness, you can't put a money value on it. Even if you can, it doesn't mean you will feel safer after you have that amount of money.

Fear Creates Financial Insecurity

Security has to do with your mind set and belief system. If you believe you are lacking in money, no matter how much money you make, you will still feel insecure. On the contrary, if you believe what you have now is adequate, and you trust you will able to monetize your passion eventually, you will feel secure even if you are making very little now.

Your beliefs are mostly formed from your personal or parents' experiences. If you grew up in a poor family, you might believe that money is scarce or making money is difficult. But basing your future on your past experiences is not accurate. It is just a speculation. The circumstances have already changed. There are more opportunities and resources now. It is not meaningful to compare the past with what your future can be.

> *Security is a fear-based concept*
> *while passion is a love-based concept.*

Your limiting beliefs on money make you worry and fuel your fear. Fear, in turn, makes you feel insecure financially. Worrying about financial security is a great indicator that you need to grow more *personally* than *financially*. Having more money will not cure your fear. Instead, address your fear first and build a better relationship with money.

What Is Your Relationship with Money?

You can have a job that pays really well, but without smart money habits you are going to be poor. Your money habits tell you a lot about your relationship with money. For example:

- If you run out of money constantly and have no idea what you spend it on, you are careless with money.
- If you hate spending money, you are afraid of losing money and are controlled by money.
- If you keep buying things that are unnecessary, you believe that money can buy you happiness.
- If you don't save regularly, you don't want to be controlled or denied by money.
- If you are obsessed with making money, you believe that money can solve everything.

To have a better relationship with money, pay attention to how you spend your money and change your money habits.

Choosing a Job Based on Prospects Is Risky

Jobseekers and graduates pick their careers and majors based on:

- Industry prospects and income
- Strengths and talents
- Interests and passions

Most people look for jobs that give them the best prospects and income because of social conditioning and their parents' influence. They believe these jobs are more stable and can give them a better life. But contrary to what they think, choosing career paths based on industry prospects is actually the most risky route to go. Here's why.

1. Industry prospects change all the time.

During my time in university, the biomedical field was deemed the most employable industry. Many people decided to have biomedical majors because of that. However, when I graduated, the biomedical industry wasn't that attractive anymore. Aerospace engineering became the most employable industry instead.

And this situation didn't necessarily occur because of inaccurate predictions about industry prospects. It is just that, in general, it takes someone three to four years to get a degree. The industry might have a manpower shortage at the time you are studying. But by the time you have graduated, the needs might have already been filled. The industry doesn't need to hire anymore people.

All industries have certain peak-and-lull periods. The industry needs more manpower when it is just starting out or in its growth stage. It won't be hiring as many employees when it reaches its mature stage.

2. You have no control over industry prospects.

No one can predict how an industry will change in the long run. It depends on many factors—such as the consumers, the economy, and the technology. Industries are constantly evolving to keep up with these changes.

When I was a kid, the music industry used to do well in CD sales. But after the technology improved and the Internet developed, the CD model didn't work anymore. You don't know how an industry is going to change. It's very risky to choose a career solely based on industry prospects.

Choosing Security over Love Gives You Bad Returns

Security Keeps You Stagnant

Staying in a stable job you dislike might seem worth it in the short run because of financial security. But in the long run, it moves you backwards.

Stability doesn't help you to grow. Even if you are earning a better salary, you are unlikely to be happy or improve yourself in a job you dislike. What you gain financially is negated by your unhappiness. There is no growth overall.

Not having any growth over time
is a bad investment.

Furthermore, doing something you dislike for long periods increases your expenses unnecessarily. It's unhealthy to force yourself to work. Part of your salary will be used in areas that you have neglected, like your health. Or you might need to spend more money on creature comforts to recuperate, such as taking a very expensive, luxurious holiday cruise that you really can't afford. If you are happy at work, you don't have to spend any more money to make yourself happy. You are already happy.

Passion Moves You Forward

Most people believe it's not worth sacrificing their salary to get a job they love. What they fail to see is that doing what you love as a career is a good, long-term strategy.

Not only are you doing what you love, you are also getting paid. Even though the salary might not be as much as what you would have earned doing something you dislike, at least you are happy doing what you love. Having two components of your life moving in the same positive direction gives you a better overall gain. You're not doing anything contradictory.

Time Is Valuable

You can't earn back the time you have lost.

Doing something you love is the best way to spend your time. Trading time for money is a bad investment because money can still be earned after you spend it. But you can only spend—and waste—time.

Putting a Dollar Value on Love and Security

I've said previously that you can't put a dollar value on security. But for those number nerds out there like me who are not convinced that love gives you a better return than security, let's have some fun with numbers.

Let's be mathematical for a while.

Example
Person A works for money. He does a job that he absolutely hates. He earns $50,000 annually. Happiness at work is worth $10,000 to him. Due to his work, he gets frequently depressed and tired. Each year, he spends $5,000 to get his health back to its original state and another $5,000 on shopping for

---

comfort items like food and clothing to make him happy.

Person B works for passion. He does a job that he absolutely loves. He earns $25,000 annually. Happiness at work is worth $10,000 to him, too. Due to his work, he feels happy and energetic. He doesn't need to spend additional amounts on health and comfort items.

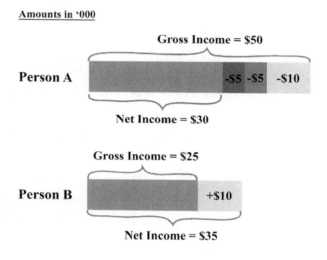

Figure 4.1 Better returns for someone who pursues passion for his career.

From Figure 4.1, you can see that a person who chooses love gets better returns. Of course, this is a hypothetical example. You can't really measure happiness.

And I'm not saying that a person who works for passion does not spend any money on health, travel, or food. I'm just saying that he does not need to spend *additional* amounts of money to get his original state of health and happiness back.

Applying Directing Techniques to Maslow's Hierarchy of Needs

Being a film director, you are responsible for the overall vision of the film. You need to make sure all the lighting, acting, staging, and camera movement work with one another. You look at everything as a whole.

You cannot have dim lighting that conveys a sad, dramatic mood while an actor performs a comedic routine; the two will clash. No matter how good the actor's acting is, the lighting is not going to bring out what he wants to convey; it will drag the quality of the film down. You need to have everything work with each other and aligned with your vision for a movie to work.

It's the same in how you live your life. Everything has to move in the same direction toward your vision. If something is moving in an opposing direction, it will drag the quality of your life down.

Seeing Maslow's Hierarchy of Needs Like a Director

Abraham Maslow was an American psychologist. He was renowned for creating Maslow's hierarchy of needs. The hierarchy states that there are five levels of needs that motivate people. The first four levels (physiological, safety, love, and esteem) are basic needs. The theory suggests you need to fulfill your basic needs first before you can achieve the fifth need (self-actualization).

Which Level Do Financial Security and Passion Belong in?

Financial security belongs to the second level of needs (safety). Being employed and having monthly income make you feel safe.

Pursuing your passion belongs to the fifth level of needs (self-actualization). You seek to realize your full potential.

Figure 4.2 Maslow's hierarchy of needs.

When I look at Maslow's hierarchy of needs, I don't see it as a level-by-level progression. Although it's important to satisfy your basic needs first, I prefer to see the hierarchy as a whole like a director.

If I am to ultimately actualize myself, why not align my basic needs with my passion right from the start? I can get a job that satisfies both my financial needs and passion rather than a job I dislike but pays well, only to realize much later on that it doesn't satisfy my self-actualization needs. Otherwise, wouldn't that be a waste of my time, resources, and money?

Also, meeting basic needs only gives you instant gratification. It only satisfies you in the short-term.

Being stuck at the basic-needs level means
you are just surviving, not living.

In the long run, you are not living up to your true potential. It is only when you work toward your full potential that you will have happiness and meaning in your life. It is more useful to consider all the levels together, instead of getting stuck at one level and trying to fulfill that need.

If you kept wanting financial security, when would you give yourself the permission to do what you love?

Do You Really Want to Do Something Uninspiring?

At the end of the day, it's not about making money. You can receive money from many avenues, such as a job, business, stocks, lottery, and a family inheritance. What matters most is where you want to make money from. Making money out of what you love doing is a lot more fun and rewarding.

"Work without love is slavery." — Mother Teresa

I'm not encouraging you to leave you job immediately and make a career change. But since you spend most of your waking hours in your job, would you rather do something you enjoy and are proud of? Or would you rather do something you hate?

When you choose to do something you love, no matter what obstacles you face, no matter what beliefs and fears you have, there will always be solutions.

If you are still hanging onto a job you hate, ask yourself: "Do I really want to do something uninspiring?"

Chapter 5

OTHER HIDDEN FEARS YOU NEED TO UNCOVER

PETER YANG DIDN'T HAVE A CONCRETE IDEA for his business when he submitted his resignation letter. He trusted his inspiration and the dots started to connect as he progressed.

Three years ago, Peter was a senior manager at a major consulting firm in Singapore. He had been working there for more than eight years, helping public and private sectors finance their infrastructure projects. But for two years, he had been asking the same question: *"What else can I do?"*

Despite doing very well in his job and getting double-promoted twice, being a partner of the firm was not what he hoped to achieve. He wanted to make a difference in society and do something more meaningful instead. But he didn't know how until he had a spiritual awakening.

One day, as Peter was lying in his bed and listening to a module from Oprah and Eckhart Tolle's course, *A New Earth*, he heard a voice while half-awake. The voice asked him to set up an organization to help charities be more effective. At that moment, he knew this idea was going to work. He had no fear. Nothing was going to stop him. He was ready to resign.

That, however, only lasted for two days.

Being too smart creates fears.

When Peter began to rationalize the inspiration he received, fears crept in. What if the inspiration is not real? What if it's just something he made up in his mind? What if it didn't work? He talked to his friends, but no one had had a similar experience. None of them could validate his inspiration.

He realized that he wouldn't know if his idea would work or not unless he tried it out himself. So he decided to resign and his organization, Empact, was born.

Connecting the Dots

Empact is a social enterprise that provides key operational services like accounting and human resources to other nonprofit and social organizations. Leveraging volunteers' skills, it's able to bring professional services to the nonprofits at affordable rates.

But these ideas weren't formed out of nothing. They were created by experiences Peter had accumulated over the years. For example:

- He had had a passion for volunteering since his university days.
- His boss asked him to get an accounting qualification one day. He didn't like the idea. It was not related to his

work, but he did it anyway. His accounting degree later became useful in his business.

- Having several friends running social enterprises, he noticed they felt demoralized and overwhelmed with non-core duties such as accounting. His business idea came while trying to address this problem.
- Already knowing people in the sector, it was easier for him to ask potential clients what they needed.

But perhaps one of his most valuable experiences was his hospice visit five years ago. He was dragged along by a friend to volunteer at the last minute and he wasn't prepared for it. During the visit, they were assigned to a patient in the last stage of her life. Their job was to make her feel better.

Despite all his financial knowledge, Peter didn't know what to say to her. She was having dialysis and had tubes all over her body. She was screaming in pain. There was nothing Peter could say or do to comfort her. He couldn't remove her from the physical pain. During the whole process, he felt he added no value to the patient.

Peter had been volunteering in various activities, but this was the first time he thought about adding value. He realized he could contribute more with his professional skills instead. And this later triggered his idea of using volunteers for his business.

Steve Jobs said you could only connect the dots looking backward. That was what Peter did. He trusted that the dots would connect in the future one day, and they did.

Key Lessons from Peter's Story

1. Use meaningless experiences to create meaningful experiences.

Peter didn't know why he volunteered so much in the past. He just loves to learn new skills and wants to know how society operates. He also didn't see any point in studying accounting, but he did it anyway.

Once he started Empact, all his past experiences became useful. He told me:

> "Whatever I've accumulated in the past seems pointless, but when it all comes together, it becomes meaningful."

Not everything you do in life must have a return. What's meaningless to you now can be such a gift to you tomorrow. Some things are meant to be used later in life. Just follow your intuition and trust the dots will connect somehow in the future.

2. You are fearless until you start to rationalize.

Peter was confident about his inspiration for two days before he started rationalizing it and then his fears kicked in. Everyone has this inner knowing of what is best for them. But when you let your intellect interfere and question your inspiration with "what ifs," it leaves you in doubt.

**Rationalizing seems to protect you from harm,
but it actually harms you more
by stopping you from being your best self.**

There's no way to know if an idea will work or not until you test it out. An idea that can be validated has already been used before by someone. There is nothing new or special about that idea. Inspirations that are given to you are meant to be pursued by you. If you fail to act on them, your ideas will be given to someone else.

3. Communicating your fears to other people helps to dissolve them.

Peter has a habit of sharing his fears with his friends. When he was having doubts in setting up a business, he consulted his friends for advice. And even though he didn't get any answers, at least he became clear that he needed to try it out himself to find out if it would work or not.

Peter also shared with me he had a fear of failure after Empact was created. And it wasn't because he was afraid of failure per se. He was more afraid of how he would appear to others when he failed.

Would other people consider him a failure?

As usual, he communicated his fears to others. His friends told him that they would never think less of him even if his business failed. In fact, they thought he was brave to pursue his passion.

Fear focuses on you. It seldom focuses on the issue itself. It's always:

- I'm not going to have enough money.
- I'll disappoint my friends and family.
- I'll look bad if I fail.

Talking to others helps to bring a different perspective to

> your fears. Peter understood that if his business failed, it didn't mean he failed. He was able to detach himself from his business with the help of his friends. Sharing your fears allow you to step outside of yourself for a moment and address your fears objectively.

Fears You Don't Even Know You Have

In the last chapter, I talked about the biggest fear about pursuing your passion—financial security. In this chapter, I'll be sharing eight other fears:

1. Fear of failure
2. Fear of success
3. Fear of being laughed at
4. Fear of uncertainty
5. Far of making mistakes
6. Fear of commitment
7. Fear of rejection
8. Fear of disappointing others

Some of them might not be so obvious to you at first. But if you identify with any fears as you read this chapter, I suggest you write them down. It will be helpful for the exercises in chapter 6. And remember, being aware of your fears is already a big step to becoming fearless.

Sometimes, it's hard to define fears into one specific category as they tend to overlap with each other. It's not a big deal if you can't categorize your fear. Categorizing the fear only helps to verbalize it. You can write down exactly what you are afraid of instead and start from there.

What's important is to clearly know what are you afraid of that stops you from taking action on your passion.

Fear #1: Fear of Failure

I notice something interesting. Whenever a host asks for volunteers to participate in a game on stage, hardly anyone will volunteer. You don't see people rushing to the stage to participate. Instead, people would rather recommend their friends go on stage instead of themselves.

Why?

Because no one wants to fail in front of others. It's shameful. If you aren't good at something, no one will know it except you. But if you go on stage, you are letting everyone know that you aren't good at it.

Failure is not as scary when you don't fail in front of others.

Most people don't want to look bad in front of their bosses, parents, and peers. Failure affects their self-image, identity, and reputation. That's why many want to avoid failure at all cost.

However, if you think about it, there is actually nothing shameful about failing. Everyone fails at least once in life, especially when doing something new for the first time. Failure is just feedback that something isn't working.

Failure Means Please Try Again

The point of failing is so you can figure out how to be successful the next time. Don't take it personally. **Failing is necessary to be successful.**

Here are three examples of how to *objectively* accept failure instead of *personally*:

	When taken personally:	When taken objectively:
I failed in my business because...	I'm not good enough to be an entrepreneur.	The timing wasn't right.
I failed my driving test because...	I'm a bad driver.	I didn't practice enough.
I failed to resolve this problem because...	I must be stupid and not creative enough.	The method I used was incorrect.

When you pursue your passion and you fail, just try again. Similar to a scientist doing an experiment, keep changing the variables (the method, resources, skills, etc.) one at a time until you succeed.

It's Not Possible to Fail

Every passion is worth pursuing. You always gain something valuable out of pursuing your passion, such as joy and the experiences you accumulate from doing what you love.

You can't possibly fail when you pursue your passion. If you are passionate about baking and you want to open your own bakery, but you bake a batch of burnt cookies when you practice, you won't have failed. You would have learned that something was wrong with your procedures. You would have gained experience and know what not to do the next time. You are moving one step toward your goal of opening a bakery. You won't make the same mistake when you open the bakery. Time was not wasted. So how can you fail?

No matter what you do, it's impossible to fail **unless you give up at the point of failure.** The faster you fail and the faster you get back up and try again, the faster you learn how to be successful.

- **Learning something new**

I started learning how to ride a bicycle only at the age of nineteen. The first time I rode it, I couldn't stop it in time. I ended up hitting a curb and hurting my knee. The second time I rode, I couldn't control it again, and I fell into the bush.

I could have given up after these two attempts and said that I couldn't ride a bicycle, but I didn't. These failed attempts gave me a better grasp of how to control my speed and when to start slowing down before I crushed into something. And after the two falls, I finally knew how to ride a bicycle.

- **Taking part in a competition**

The same song I used to win a regional songwriting competition did not even make it past the semifinal in another competition. The same song in two different competitions gave me two different results. If I had given up on my song the first time I failed, I would never have won the other competition.

From my failure, I learned that I needed to rehearse with my singer more so that he could remember the lyrics. I realized I needed someone to do the background vocals and play the piano instead of using a prearranged, minus-one tape. I made use of stage lighting the second time around to bring out the visual aspects of the performance.

I only knew what it took to win after I had failed.

***

If you are teaching your child how to say "mommy" and "daddy," and he fails on the first try, do you give up on your child and not teach him anymore? No, because you believe he can do it. If you bring the same faith to your passion, one day you will be successful.

Failing once doesn't mean you are a failure for life. There's always a chance to be successful if you keep trying. **The only way to fail is to stop trying.**

If you give up when you fail, you'll always remain at the point where you stop trying, which is failure. What's important after each failure is:

- What you have learned from it, and
- How you pick yourself up after it.

Fear #2: Fear of Success

Not everyone wants to be successful.

Fear of success might be confusing to some people. Why would anyone not want to be successful?

Well, the basic assumption that everyone loves themselves is false. Not everyone loves themselves and feels that they are worthy to be successful. Not everyone believes they deserve to do the work they love. And this is apparent when someone constantly worries about how others might think of them and react to their success (or failure).

You deserve to be successful and do what you love. If you are going to lose your friends or loved ones because they are jealous of your success, I think you are better off without them. Don't feel guilty for being successful.

Fumbling before You Finish

When I was in Primary School, there was a track-and-field meet every year. For the first two years, I was selected by my teacher to participate in one of the events. But somehow when the actual event got closer, I would fumble at the practice session and be replaced by another classmate. It happened to me twice.

I didn't understand why I always fumbled toward the end. I thought that I was just pure unlucky and I was always envious of those who participated in the track-and-field meet. During my fourth year in school, I finally made it to the actual event, and my team came in second.

After the event, I understood why I fumbled the first two times. I was afraid of not doing well in the actual meet. It was pretty nerve-wracking to participate in the actual meet. I didn't want to be the one who made a mistake and brought my whole team down.

Being successful at the rehearsals would mean that I had to participate in the actual event. And that freaked me out. So I sabotaged my performance during rehearsals so that I would be replaced.

***

Success can be scary because of the changes it brings—more challenges, pressure, and responsibilities. Sometimes, people don't want to perform well at work because they are worried that they will be given more work. And being afraid of success can cause performance anxiety and self-sabotage.

Most of the time, people sabotage themselves without even knowing it. If you aren't getting the results you desire in life, you probably should ask yourself:

What am I doing that
prevents me from being happy?

Is what I'm doing not working, or am I afraid of being successful?

Fear #3: Fear of Being Laughed At

There is no harm in sharing what you love.

I didn't talk in secondary school. I was known as the "boring" person. Every time my teacher asked me to recite a passage in the textbook, my classmates would keep quiet so that they could hear me speak. One classmate even joked that the number of words he spoke in one day was more than the number of words I had spoken for four years.

I used to be very afraid to share what I loved. I felt that others would judge me for being different. I studied in a boy's school. Most of my classmates were active and loved sports like soccer. On the other hand, I was more reserved and loved writing songs and designing web banners.

There was no one like me.

To protect myself from being the class "Dumbo," I chose not to share my passions. But later I found it tiring to worry about what others thought of me all the time. So I started opening up in junior college.

I was a huge fan of the reality TV show *Survivor* then. (Still am today!) I remember in my class I set up a small corner at the whiteboard for *Survivor*. Each week, I would write who was voted out and what could be expected for next week. One time, my economics teacher came in, saw my *Survivor* corner, and commented on the show. She didn't like it. She didn't like that the contestants in the show had to lie, backstab, and vote each other out.

But I wasn't bothered by her comments at all.

I was able to separate her opinions of the show from my self-image. I knew she hated the show, but that didn't mean she hated me. Also, loving *Survivor* didn't mean I condoned lying and backstabbing. I was not a liar for loving *Survivor!*

At the end of my two years in junior college, everyone in class knew me as the *Survivor* guy. People would discuss the show with me. And I naturally opened up more when I talked about the show. I definitely became more sociable because of that. I was no longer the "boring" person.

I guess sharing your passion—whatever it is— is not that bad after all.

***

No one wants to be made fun of like The Ugly Ducking or Dumbo. But don't hide your passion just because you are afraid that others will laugh at you. Be proud of your passion and share it with the world. The world needs your passion.

There's No Meaning in Laughter

If you know me, you will know that I have a very "horrible" laugh. My friend once told me she can locate me in the office with my loud, distinct laughter. And I laugh all the time! I laugh when I'm happy. I laugh when I'm nervous. I laugh when I make a mistake.

Laughing should be good for you. It helps to release stress. But why are people so bothered by laughter itself?

> *People who are afraid of being laughed at*
> *are afraid of being judged by others.*

People aren't really bothered by laughter itself. What really bothers them are the meanings they attach to other people's laughter:

- "You want to be an actress. Maybe you should look at yourself in the mirror."
- "That is a stupid idea for a business. It won't work."
- "Giving up a well-paid job for your passion—how foolish is that?"

When people see laughter as mockery, it makes them feel inferior, dumb, and shameful in front of others.

Don't assign meanings to other people's laughter. The meaning you assign it might be spot-on or totally untrue. You can't tell. So why bother interpreting it in your mind? It's a total waste of time and energy.

Have the First Laugh, Not Just the Last laugh

The best way to be free from being laughed at is to learn to laugh at yourself first.

When you laugh at yourself first, you have the first-mover advantage. You don't give other people the opportunity to laugh at you. You are sending them a message, "I know it's dumb, but I love it." Most people don't laugh at people who are already laughing at themselves!

More importantly, have a sense of humor. Life doesn't have to be so serious all the time. Laugh at how crazy your dreams are. Laugh at how unrealistic and silly you are. Laugh at how different and brave you are. When you are able to laugh at yourself first, you can't be bothered by what other people think of you.

Fear #4: Fear of Uncertainty

The unknown makes you feel uncomfortable and powerless. It gets you out of your comfort zone. When you know what is going to happen next, you can prepare for it. When you don't know what to expect, you cannot rely on your past experience. You have to adjust yourself accordingly to the circumstances.

But life is unpredictable. **Uncertainty is the only certainty.** It's unrealistic to think you can control every event and outcome:

- You can't control other people's actions.
- You can't control external events.
- You can't control what others think of you.

You Can Only Control Yourself

One of my friends asked me what if I couldn't sell any copies of this book. Wouldn't I have wasted my money, time, and effort?

Well, I can't control whether people are going to buy this book or not. What I can control are the quality of this book and how I market it. My responsibilities are to write the best book that I can write and bring the message to the readers who need it. Whether someone buys my book or not is not something I can control. So why worry about something that I don't have control over? If I have zero sales, then I will have to ask myself where did it go wrong and try some different marketing and publicity strategies.

You can choose to be affected by unfavorable events, or you can stay focused on your goals and move on. Don't waste your time on things you can't control; focus on the things you can.

The less reactive you are to external events, the more control you have internally.

Uncertainty Can Give You Hope

The death of Swamiji's parents opened up his spiritual life.

When Swamiji was a freshman in college majoring in TV and film, he lost his parents in a car accident. Even though he loved his major, he quickly lost interest in his studies. To cope with the grief and angst he was dealing with, he began to study yoga and meditation. They gave him the inner serenity he needed.

However, after working in the TV industry for a few years, Swamiji felt something was missing from his life. He felt depressed. The world was empty for him.

He had not truly resolved his parents' death.

At that time, Swamiji was reading about Ayurveda (the Indian healing system). He had a vision to open his own Ayurveda herb shop, but he had no experience in running a business. Ayurveda was also pretty much unknown in America at that time, and he had to study it in India.

Swamiji was afraid of the unknown. But he knew that if he continued to stay in his job, his depression was going to get worse. The fear of the unknown was easier to deal with than the known that he didn't want to deal with. The unknown was the lesser of two evils.

At least the unknown gave him hope.

So, he went to India and began spiritual studies with his guru. Later, he became a monk and was finally at peace. Now, his biggest passion is to help people heal instantly and awaken to their inner joy—something that he had been seeking ever since his parents died in the car crash.

***

If you are in an unpleasant emotional state like Swamiji was, the best thing you can do for yourself is to make a change. Even if there are uncertainties in the change, at least there is a chance that it will be better than your current state. If you don't do anything, you are just going to remain stuck where you are now.

Uncertainty can be beautiful. Learn to see its beauty. When you don't know what will happen next, enjoy the freedom to choose your action spontaneously. Life isn't fun when everything is so predictable.

Fear #5: Fear of Making Mistakes

The fear of making mistakes is somewhat similar to the fear of uncertainty. People who are afraid of making mistakes tend to plan excessively to make sure that all the uncertainties are covered. I am guilty of that.

I love to plan and I think that planning is absolutely necessary in most cases. But sometimes, I do plan a little too much and take too long to start something. For example, I will take a long time to choose what WordPress template to use for my website. And just the other day, my brother was laughing at me because I was planning an exercise regime to pass my fitness test.

He suggested, "Why don't you just exercise now instead."

Always Make U-Turns when You Are Wrong

I'm thankful that I picked an unsuitable career for myself at the start of my working life. It made me seek a clearer career path. If I didn't become an auditor, I probably wouldn't have known that I needed to do something meaningful as a career. And I probably wouldn't be writing this book to encourage others to pursue their passions. Doing something I disliked showed me the importance of doing what I loved.

Although accounting is not my passion, I still learned a lot from it. During my five years in the finance industry, I learned problem-solving skills, communication skills, and time-management skills, which are all very beneficial to my future career.

People tell me that I have wasted my accounting degree and experience. But to me, I feel that if I had continued down that wrong career path, I was just going to waste more time. I can now use this time to develop a career that I love instead.

So why not make a U-turn?

***

If you are driving on a road and you make a wrong turn, what do you do? Do you continue to go down the wrong path? No, you make a U-turn and get back to the correct path. You don't continue driving down the wrong path and getting farther away from your destination.

It's the same in life. If you make a mistake or pick a wrong career, just make a U-turn. What's lost is lost, you can't get it back. What you can focus on is the path ahead and the destination you desire to reach.

You Don't Have to Be Perfect Every Time

Trying to be perfect all the time is tough. You create unnecessary stress and ironically, you become more prone to making mistakes. The fear of making mistakes prevents you from reaching your potential. To avoid mistakes, you continue to do what has previously worked for you. But the previous method might not be the best and most efficient method.

Being imperfect gives you the opportunity to learn and grow. Give yourself the freedom to make mistakes and be more open to new ideas. You are more likely to generate creative ideas to solve an existing problem.

Fear #6: Fear of Commitment

The fear of commitment comes from the fear of losing something valuable. People are afraid that they will lose their freedom, time, money, options, and so on if they commit to something. This is a misconception. The truth is **commitments aren't restrictive.**

Even if you commit to something now, you can always change it later. Changing doesn't mean giving up or breaking your promise. It just means that you are reassessing the situation and seeing that there are better opportunities out there that suit your needs more. You don't have to stick to something if it doesn't align to what you want anymore.

If you decide to change, recommit again. Don't blame yourself for changing or being fickle. It's like when you sign a contract with someone and you decide to change some of the terms later, just draft out an amendment to supersede the terms in the previous contract. Commitment just means you put in your best effort and focus to complete what you want to accomplish at that moment. It's not binding forever.

Commitment Gives You Freedom

Remember in chapter 4 where I shared that I went back to work part-time for my ex-company for the second time?

Well, I resigned after working for two months after I went back there the second time. It was when I interviewed Simon Gudgeon (from chapter 2) that I realized I had forgotten what I was truly committed to—animation. What he said about committing to your passion fully and don't be half-hearted about it really struck a chord with me and woke me up.

Why aren't I spending time doing animation right now? Aren't I arrogant for not improving my animation skills and expecting companies to hire me when I have not grown at all? Am I afraid of committing to animation, or am I just easily distracted?

After reflecting, I decided to quit my job and free up my precious time to improve my animation skills and demo reel. I told my boss that I won't be doing accounting or auditing ever again. There is no backup for animation. Animation is what I truly wanted. No matter how hard it is or how afraid I am, I have to give it my all and make it work.

It felt liberating to commit to what I love.

***

Contrary to what most people think, commitment actually gives you freedom instead of taking it away from you. When you commit to something, you don't waste time doing something else that isn't important to you. Commitment frees up your time for important things in life. If you aren't committed, though, you get distracted easily.

For example, I was distracted by the opportunity to earn extra income. Even writing this book was a distraction to me. I haven't been animating much since I graduated in December of 2013 because I was so caught up with this book. I forgot that I want to be an animator who writes, not an author who only does animation during his free time.

Before you commit to something, you already have the freedom to choose. Not committing to anything doesn't mean that you continue to have that freedom. It just means you are not using the freedom you have. **What use is freedom to choose when you don't choose?**

Fear #7: Fear of Rejection

Everyone wants to be part of a group. Being accepted makes you feel valued. Being rejected invalidates you. Your self-worth depends on how others see you, or rather, how you see others see you.

You Should Not Reject Yourself First

Sometimes, people overthink about what others think of them. Don't reject yourself first by assuming that others will reject you. There are people out there who are willing to support your dreams and aspirations. Most of the time, it isn't as bad as you think.

- **It's not a rejection when you are not formally rejected.**

I've sent out over twenty interview requests to get stories for this book, but only half of them replied. I did felt a little rejected at first. They could at least replied "no" so that I know they are not interested and I can move on to the next person. But then I thought to myself, perhaps they were too busy, they might have missed the e-mail, or the e-mail might have ended up in their spam folder. And that made me feel better.

Truly enough, one of them replied to me three weeks later and apologized for the late reply. My e-mail had ended up in her spam mail. I wasn't rejected. My e-mail was just not read. And even if they had ignored my e-mails, I shouldn't take it personally.

Rejecting your request is not the same as rejecting you as a person. There could be so many other reasons why they had ignored you. Don't make up bad reasons about yourself.

- **People are more supportive of your dream than you think they are.**

Anne (more about her in chapter 11) shared with me that she was very nervous about tendering her resignation letter. She was afraid of how her bosses and colleagues would respond.

Would they think she was crazy to leave her job for a career break?

It turned out that all their responses were very nice. Her bosses understood what she was doing and they didn't try to change her mind. Some of her colleagues even thought that she was very brave to pursue what she wanted.

Nothing really bad happened the way she had imagined.

***

Of course, there will always be people who are going to reject you and your dreams. But you don't need everyone's approval to do what you love. If you get rejected, just move onto the next person. Just seek other people who are encouraging and share the same passions as you.

Fear #8: Fear of Disappointing Others

The feeling of disappointment comes from failing to meet expectations. Your parents' expectations of you to get a stable job and make a good income can make you feel guilty if you decide to pursue your own passion. If you oppose them, it feels like you are upsetting them and not being filial.

Stop Trying to Meet Other People's Expectations

As much as you love your parents, you cannot help them to manage their expectations. You are not the cause of their disappointment. Everyone is responsible for their own happiness. You don't have the power to make everyone happy. Don't sacrifice your happiness just to please them.

Ask yourself:

Whose life are you living?
Yours or theirs?

Their expectations are formed by their beliefs, and beliefs are neither true nor false; it's just what society generally thinks is good or bad.

Some examples of beliefs are:

- Getting a stable job is good.
- Money is more important than passion.
- You cannot make a living doing what you love.

There is no right or wrong when it comes to pursuing your passion. Just choose the path that makes you happy. The more you force yourself to do what your parents want, the more likely you will feel resentment toward them.

Just be yourself!

Chapter 6

HOW TO HARNESS YOUR FEARS

WHEN APPLYING FOR HIS FIRST JOB, Dan Conway never stood a chance. Not only did he have to compete with other graduates, entry-level jobs were quickly snapped up by people who are already in the field. How could a recent graduate like him match up to someone who had real-world experience?

Dan had earned a bachelor of arts degree in Creative Advertising from Leeds College of Art & Design in 2009. For four years, he was not able to find a permanent job in the industry he loves despite sending out many resumes to employers. To earn a living, he had to work as a substitute teacher and youth worker, fields unrelated to what he really wanted to do. He even tried to set up a bakery business with his wife, but it failed.

The turning point of his career came when he lost his youth-worker job one week before his wife delivered their second child. He knew he needed to do something drastic and different immediately so he could support his family of four.

Pursuing Your Passion Can Be Extreme

Dan was sick of applying for jobs in the same old boring way. It was ineffective and did not reflect his personality at all. He hardly got any responses from employers. Why not make a creative cover letter and CV instead? Anyway, being creative was something he loved to do.

So he started designing spoof cover letters with really silly messages—"I'm the best; I'm a superhero; I fight crime at night"—and sent them out to employers.

His creativity paid off! A few days later, he received a letter from one of the companies he had contacted. The employer loved his application, it made them laugh, and they wanted to interview him for the job. Though he did not get that job in the end, he realized that being different worked.

So he decided to make something even larger. He wanted to create a marketing campaign so viral and big that it would grab the attention of employers. In his mind, all he could think of was:

"I'm twenty-seven and graduated four years ago. I have to give my dream job one last shot. How much worse could it get?"

It took him a couple of months to plan the social media concept and the website. In the end, he came out with a brand called "The Extreme Job Hunter" and along with it a character that stood out with big glasses and red suspenders. Each week, he would do a crazy marketing stunt to attract potential employers, and he intended to do this until he was hired.

A few of the outlandish stunts he did included:

- Doing a topless picket on the busy streets of Newcastle to promote his website
- Entering the Gravy Wrestling Championships to get publicity
- Auctioning himself on eBay to potential employers
- Giving a free iPad Mini to anyone who helped him get a job
- Creating a visual resume starring his two-year-old daughter, Lucy

He did whatever he could to get the attention he needed to land his dream job. His new rule was never to apply for jobs in a boring way again. He was going to have fun while hunting for a new career.

Not long after his first stunt with his daughter, Lucy, the local newspaper picked up on it. Dan knew at that point that it was going to be a success. Soon, the story was picked up by local radio stations and later became a national news story when he appeared on the *BBC Breakfast Show*, the biggest breakfast show in the UK.

Five months later, the head of a US-based company, Vitamins Direct, came across his website, liked what Dan was doing, and decided to hire him. Dan's fun and creative personality were just what the company needed. Now, he is in charge of web and social media at Vitamins Direct.

All this came about because he chose to be himself.

Key Lessons from Dan's Story

1. Being yourself lands you the dream job.

Dan always knew that he loved creative marketing. It was his first choice for a career, but he was not successful at finding a job in this field. However, when he brought his passion into his job-hunting process, he found much more success in getting noticed than when he followed the conventional way of applying for jobs.

Not only that, he got to be himself in the process. This was what he said to me with regard to his viral marketing campaign:

> "I feel very liberated. I feel that I'm expressing something that is a piece of me. I'm having so much fun, but at the same time, communicating to potential employers and showing them what I can offer them."

Pursuing his passion allows Dan to be himself! It frees him. There will be people who will not like what he does, but that is okay. It just means that those employers are not the right fit for him. You want to have an employer that appreciates your personality, and expressing your passion can help you do just that.

2. Staying in your comfort zone may erode your passion.

I asked Dan a question during our interview: "If you didn't lose your job, do you think you would have been so extreme in trying new job-search strategies?" His reply was no. He had been feeling comfortable with the youth work he was doing.

It was a stable job, the money was good, and it had career progression. He would have stayed with that job if he had not been laid off. In hindsight, losing his job turned out to be a blessing, as it gave him the time to think about his career path and forced him to give his passion in advertising one last try.

Many people who do not enjoy their work do not think about it because they are getting too comfortable in their current job. Being content does not mean giving up on what you genuinely desire. You can be content with your current work, but still work toward what you love. Sometimes, being too comfortable makes you forget about what you love doing and prevents you from growing your passion to its full potential.

3. Fear is an opportunity for your courage to shine.

After losing his job, Dan could easily have gone back and done part-time work as a substitute teacher to make ends meet. Instead, he chose to take a chance and went all-out to pursue his passion for the very last time.

Whenever you are faced with fear, you have a decision to make: either let your fear paralyze you or use it to do something great and get what your heart desires. Every fear you experience is an opportunity for you to showcase the courage hidden within you. It is for you to decide what you want to do with it.

Fears Can Be Useful, Too

Most people think they need to conquer fear. Instead, I believe there is purpose in living with fear. Although fears can stop you from taking action, fears do not have to be crushed.

Fears are not your enemy.

Fear tells you where you are blocked and where you need growth. Fear tells you the areas in which you're less confident so that you can build up your confidence in those areas.

Whenever you approach a new stage in your life, you will have new fears. You can't get rid of your fears completely. When you are a student, you worry whether you'll do well in your exams. When you graduate, you will be afraid that you won't get a job. When you are an employee, you are afraid you won't perform well in your job. Your old fears subside whenever you take actions and new fears emerge.

Fears are here to **mark your growth and transition** to the next stage. So instead of battling with fears, you should think of ways to use them to your advantage.

Method #1: Question Yourself

Objective: To figure out what you are really afraid of.

Sometimes, fears are formed by negative events you think you have let go of. You might not be aware that you are still holding onto them. Whenever you are afraid to take action, it's helpful to question yourself and examine the root of your fears. Don't

believe what you tell yourself at face value. Question further
and identify the fear behind your excuses. Be specific about
your fear. The clearer you can be about your fear, the less scary
it is. Gauge what's at stake and whether it is reasonable to be
fearful of it.

Here are a few questions you can ask yourself when you
find it difficult to take action on what you love:

- What am I telling myself right now?
  (*Sample answer: I do not have the time right now.*)

- Is it the truth or is there another reason? Am I making
  up any excuses?
  (*Sample answer: Well, I can stop playing my games right
  now and work on my passion, but I don't know where to
  start.*)

- Is there something I am afraid of?
  (*Sample answer: I afraid if I take a wrong step, I will fail.*)

- Why am I afraid? What is at stake here?
  (*Sample answer: If I fail, I might waste an hour or two.*)

- Considering what is at stake, is it reasonable to be
  afraid?
  (*Sample answer: I guess it is okay to spend an hour on my
  passion.*)

- If there is too much at stake, is there any way I can
  minimize the stake?
  (*Sample answer: An hour is too much. Perhaps I will just
  spend half an hour to see how it goes.*)

Method #2: Treat It Like a Game

Objective: To make fear fun.

Every fear you have is a challenge to your personal growth. Similar to playing a game, there is a bigger challenge to tackle on the next level. If you can have so much fun playing computer games and clearing levels, why can't you have fun with your fears, too?

Let's take singing as an example.

Comfort Level	Fear Encounter
Level 1 – Singing to yourself in the bathroom	Afraid of singing in front of others
Level 2 – Singing in front of a family member	Afraid of singing in front of friends
Level 3 – Singing in front of friends	Afraid of singing on stage in front of strangers
Level 4 – Singing on a small stage	Afraid of singing on a large stage in front of thousands people

A person who first starts singing is afraid to sing in front of others. Every time he takes action toward his passion, his old fear disappears and a new one emerges. So why not treat your fears like a game?

Every new fear you have simply means you have reached a new stage of growth and new obstacles are presented to challenge you. You can take up the challenge and learn from it, or you can ignore it and remain stuck at your level. It all depends on you. Give yourself rewards and brownie points for completing each level like you would in a real game. Celebrate!

Method #3: Get the Best View

Objective: To perceive fear in a way that best serves you.

Getting the best view is about shifting your perception toward fear. Successful people are successful because of how they perceive fear. They don't see fear as something that is unfavorable; they see fear as an opportunity to grow. You can shift your perception easily, too. *You can't choose your fears, but you can choose how you view your fears.*

Imagine you're in a crowd watching a performance on stage. If someone tall stands in front of you and blocks your view, what do you do?

A. Simply shift yourself to the left or the right and get another view of the stage, or
B. Continue to stand behind the tall person and get angry or upset with that person.

Shifting perception is as simple as moving yourself to another position. It does not take much effort at all. You can stand at the center, right, or left of the stage. The view is somewhat different, but the performance is the same.

Choosing (B) doesn't help you watch the performance at all. You are just wasting your energy on the person in

> front of you. But that's what most people do. When fear blocks them, they allow it to affect them and hinder their actions. But all they have to do is reposition themselves.

When fear paralyzes you from taking action, ask yourself:

- How can I see my fear in a positive light?
- How can I perceive my fear in a way that best serves me?
- How can I position myself so that I can harness the fear to move toward what I want?
- What gifts are there in my fears that I fail to see?

Remember, your goal is to watch the performance. Your focus should be on pursuing your passion, not the fear standing in front of you. You can see fear as an obstacle that blocks your view or an opportunity to get a better view. It all depends on your perception.

Exercise

On a piece of paper, write down how you can perceive each of the following fears differently and choose your best view. In chapters 4 and 5, I've shared my views on these fears. Reread the previous two chapters to get some ideas. You can also use other fears you have for this exercise.

Fears:	My Best View:
Fear of not having enough money	e.g., Money is just a by-product to get what I love.

Fear of disappointing others	e.g., I don't have the power to upset others. Empower them to manage their own expectations.
Fear of commitment	
Fear of being laughed at	
Fear of failure	
Fear of rejection	
Fear of uncertainty	
Fear of making mistakes	
Fear of success	

Method #4: Conduct a Fair Trial

Objective: To challenge what your fears tell you and identify areas of growth.

Most of your fears come from limiting self-beliefs. Your fears say you lack the capability to do what you love and you believe them. Don't accept everything that your fears tell you. It seems as though they are trying to protect you from harm, but they are actually scared of your growth. **Growth weakens fear.**

So next time fear tells you something, take it to court instead and conduct a fair trial. Listen to both sides of the story, challenge your beliefs, and uncover the lies that your fear tells you. Use this three-step approach:

1. Identify what your fears tell you.
2. Create a rebuttal statement against what they tell you.
3. Produce a final verdict by identifying the areas you need growth in.

Here are three examples of how you can challenge your fears using the three-step approach:

Example 1

What your fears tell you - I've tried. It's no use. No one will pay me for my passion.

Rebuttal statement - I've tried and failed several times, but it doesn't mean that I won't get paid the next time. I did not get paid previously because I didn't find a way to add value to others.

Verdict - Expand my business knowledge. Find new ways to add value with my passions and learn from others.

Example 2

What your fears tell you - I can't commit to my passion because I always lose my interests pretty fast.

Rebuttal statement - I can commit to my passion if it is really something I love to do and important to me. I couldn't commit previously because I'm not really passionate about those activities.

Verdict - Increase your self-awareness. Explore what you love to do and give it the attention it deserves.

<u>**Example 3**</u>

What your fears tell you - People are successful in pursuing their passions because they have the talent. I don't have such talent.

Rebuttal statement - People are successful because they have the skills. I can be successful in pursuing my passion, too if I acquire those skills.

Verdict - Improve your self-confidence and capability. Identify areas that I am not confident in and work on them.

Method #5: Reverse the "What Ifs"

Objective: To replace the negative outcomes you imagine with positive outcomes.

You are afraid because you believe what you imagine will come true. But the fear is only true in your mind; it's not reality. You won't know what the actual outcome is until you take action. Remember an occasion when you had anticipated something to be a disaster but it turned out fine instead? Your mind loves to exaggerate the outcome.

It is okay if your fears don't paralyze you from taking action. But if your fears prevent you from moving forward, try the following exercise to reverse your negative "what ifs."

Exercise

1. Take out a piece of paper and draw three columns. Label them as I've indicated below:

Original "what if"	Reverse "what if"	What would it be like if my reverse "what if" comes true?

2. List all the "what ifs" (i.e., all the negative outcomes you imagine when it comes to pursuing your passion) in the left column.

For example:
- What if I do not make enough money to cover my monthly expenses?
- What if I cannot find a job that relates to my passion?
- What if my spouse, family, and friends do not support my passion?
- What if I'm not good at my passion?
- What if I pick the wrong passion to pursue?

3. Next, reverse all the "what ifs" from the left column in the center column.

For example:
- What if I make enough money to cover my monthly expenses?
- What if I find a job that relates to my passion?
- What if my spouse, family, and friends support my passion?
- What if I'm good at my passion?
- What if I pick the right passion to pursue?

4. Now, the fun part. Close your eyes and imagine all your reverse "what ifs" are true. Ask yourself these questions:

- How do I feel?

  (E.g., I feel happy and energetic.)

- What do I see?

  (E.g., I see myself working with other passionate people. All of us have so much drive in our work.)

- What does it sound like?

  (E.g., my friends congratulate me for being successful. There's so much laughter in my working environment.)

- How will the people around me feel?

  (E.g., my parents are proud of me and support what I do.)

You can write it down if you want in the right column, but do not interrupt your visualization. Get as much uplifting feeling from the positive outcomes as possible.

You Are Just Being Too Positive!

Yes, some of you might think I'm being too positive here. But if you can imagine all the negative "what ifs," why not imagine all the positive "what ifs," too? I'm not saying either version is the truth. But both scenarios are possible. You can't control the outcome, but you do have the choice to be positive or negative. Why give so much weight to negativity and let it hinder you? Why not give more weight to the positivity and enjoy the good feelings it brings?

If you worry that being too positive is too much of a fantasy, try the **"Middle-Ground Approach."** See both extremes as possibilities and establish a middle ground.

For example, when you pursue your passion as a career:

- Worst-case scenario is you waste money and time on an education and can't get any job that relates to your passion. You are not able to support yourself.
- Best-case scenario is you get a job that relates to your passion and pays you well.
- Then, the middle-ground scenario can be:
  - o You get a job that relates to your passion but pay is only satisfactory, or
  - o You don't get a job that relates to your passion, but you get a job that relates to the industry of your passion.

There is always more than one possible outcome. Don't surrender yourself to the worst outcome and accept what you imagine. Explore other possibilities.

Method 6: Give Yourself a Timeout

Objective: To break free from negativity.

Most people aren't aware how negative their thoughts are. Psychiatrist Daniel G. Amen terms this "ANTs" (automatic negative thoughts). Having constant negative thoughts can be draining and depressing. You don't feel much when one little ANT bites you. But if many ANTs bite you consistently for a long period, you are going to feel the impact.

Fear feeds on negativity. The more you feed fear with your negative thoughts, the stronger it gets. Use fear as a remainder to weed out your negativity.

One way to break free from your negative thought pattern is to give your thoughts a timeout. A timeout stops your automatic-thought cycle and makes you conscious of what you are thinking now. The challenging part, though is being aware of your thoughts. Researchers said that an average person has twelve thousand to seventy thousand thoughts a day and 80 percent of them are negative. It does take some practice to get the hang of it.

The Beginner Method

This is what I do when I first start out:

- I set an hourly alarm clock on my mobile phone.
- Whenever my alarm clock rings, a message appears: "What are you thinking now?"
- I'll then ask myself:
    o "Are my thoughts serving me right now?"

o   "Am I doing something that I want to do now?"

Having a reminder hourly is very useful as it gets me in the habit of being conscious of my thoughts. It's very disruptive when you are working, but it brings you back to the present right away. Try it! You'll be surprised how many negative thoughts you have at every moment of your life.

The Amateur Method

Now that I am more conscious of my thoughts, I don't need to set alarms on my mobile phone anymore. But there are still times when I get stuck with negative-thought patterns.

For example, when I'm doing my work and I face a technical issue that I cannot resolve, I get so focused on solving the problem that I am totally oblivious of my thoughts. In such cases, what triggers me to take a timeout are my body and my emotions. Usually, my chest will tighten and I feel frustrated and stuck.

Whenever I catch myself in this state, I'll do the following:

- Give myself a 5–10 minute break.
- Stop whatever I am doing at that point.
- Rest, meditate, zone out, or empty my mind, whatever you want to call it. I just do nothing.
- Listen to any thoughts and feelings I have and let them go. Observe them, but do not react to them. Just empty them as they come.

After I give myself a timeout, I feel much calmer and I can more easily solve my problem. The purpose of the timeout is to interrupt your negative thoughts and not let them automatically run in the background. It's important to disrupt your negative thoughts because they kill your creativity and prevent you from coming up with solutions to your problems.

Method 7: Prepare More, Predict Less

Objective: To be less reactive toward uncertainty.

Since there is no way you can accurately predict the future, what you can do instead is prepare.

> *If you don't know when it's going to rain,*
> *take along an umbrella just in case.*

Fear exists because you are uncertain about something. It tells you where you are uncertain and where you need more information. Your job is to make these uncertainties more certain.

For example:

- If you are unsure the job you are pursuing is right for you, do some market research first. Ask people who are already working in the industry for advice.
- If you don't know if your products will sell, test them out first by surveying your target market. Give out free samples and ask for feedback.
- If you are hesitant about pursuing your passion as a career, start small first. Test it out by doing freelance or part-time work while you keep your current job.

Don't Fight or Take Flight—Sit!

The natural response when you see something you are fearful of is to fight or take flight. That's because you feel that it's a direct threat to your survival.

However, fears you have on pursuing your passion aren't direct threats to your survival. So, instead of the instinctive fight or flight response, *sit on it first.* Take your time to react.

Every time you are fearful about something:

Stop!

Identify

Take actions

1. **Stop!**

   Resist the urge to react to your fears immediately.

2. **Identify**

   Take a moment to figure out where the information gap is.

3. **Take actions**

   - Read up on the things you are uncertain about and bridge the information gap you have. The more you know about the thing you are fearful about, the less scary it gets.

   - Prepare for possible scenarios. Don't bank on one single scenario happening.

PART 3:
ACTING ON YOUR PASSION

Chapter 7

HOW TO IDENTIFY WHAT YOU LOVE TO DO

BEING CALLED A NERD HELPED ME find my passion for songwriting. I used to be a student who focused a lot on academic results. I was the geek who loved textbooks. When other kids were dragging their parents to the department stores to buy toys, I would drag my parents to the bookstores to buy assessment books. I loved to be graded. Even when I did badly on my tests, designing a new study strategy to improve my grades was fun for me.

I was thirteen when my teacher, Mr. Han, asked the class to clean our desks. He said he would inspect them during our exams. That day arrived. I was, as usual, answering the questions on my exam paper until Mr. Han, who was overseeing the examination, walked to my desk and asked me to stay behind after I finished the exam. It was only then I realized I hadn't cleaned my desk. I couldn't continue with my exam anymore. I hadn't brought anything to clean my desk. All I could think of was how I was going to clean it.

I didn't want to get a scolding from Mr. Han. He would

embarrass me publicly. I remembered how he brought us up one by one to the front of the classroom and ridiculed us about how poor our work was.

I didn't want to be mocked by him. So, I solved this by...panicking! I searched my pencil case and the only thing that could possibly clean my desk was an eraser. I desperately used the eraser to remove the black marks on my desk, hoping it would be clean enough before he inspected again.

After the examinations ended, other students were busy cleaning their desks with cleaning agents they had brought from home. As Mr. Han walked nearer to my desk, I pretended to clean my desk with my eraser and tried to cover parts of my desk with my pencil case. I avoided eye contact with him, but of course, I was busted.

"What do you think you are doing?" he asked me in Mandarin. And before I could even answer, he added: "Do you think you can clean the table with an eraser? You must use Jif, for goodness sake."

As if I couldn't appear any stupider, I replied: "Gin? What's Gin?"

"You're a nerd! What's Jif? It's so common. Oh my....

Other than your textbooks, do you know anything else?"

He walked away in disbelief. (Jif is a brand name of a cleaner. It's a product from Unilever.)

Later that day on my bus ride home, tears flowed down my eyes uncontrollably. I felt I was the stupidest guy in the world, not knowing what "Gin" was.

The Nerd Learns to Create

After that incident, I started reflecting:

- What else can I do apart from studying?
- What else can I achieve other than getting good grades?
- What do I love to do?

The next year, I explored my creative side. I discovered I love to draw, design, and write. Basically, I love coming out with new ideas and executing them in many different mediums.

My love for songwriting emerged when my brother and I were listening to a Chinese radio station in Singapore. There was this music segment hosted by a DJ and a famous local lyricist named Muzi (木子老师). Listeners would send in their lyrics and melody to get feedback from Teacher Muzi.

We found this program interesting and listened to it religiously each week. My elder brother, who was learning the guitar back then, sent in his songs for feedback. I wanted to join, too, but I didn't know any music instruments. Luckily for me, there were listeners who sent in melodies without lyrics. So I taped the program and started writing lyrics for their melodies.

I enjoyed the songwriting process very much. I would repeatedly listen to the melody and imagine I was the character in the song. Then, I would have tons of fun playing with words and singing the lyrics I had written.

I was excited when I sent in my handwritten lyrics to the radio station to wait for critiques. I received good reviews for my first two lyrics. But the most memorable moment was when

Teacher Muzi said to me: "If you can write with such maturity at fourteen years old, you'll be a successful lyricist by the time you turn thirty."

With his encouragement, I wrote more songs and began writing melodies, too. And from then on, my passion for songwriting just grew.

Key Lessons from My Story

1. Passion comes to you naturally.

There is no need to be fixated on finding your passion right away. It comes to you naturally. You just need to acknowledge it when it comes and act on it.

Like my passion in songwriting; I didn't plan for it. I was just listening to the radio and found a program that I felt interested in. I was an avid music listener since I was young, but songwriting wasn't something I thought I would do one day. It was definitely not something I thought I was capable of doing until I had tried it.

So don't get flustered trying to figure out what your passion is. It will be revealed to you when the time comes.

2. Every event is a gift.

Be grateful for both the positive and negative events in your life. There is greatness in both of them.

I felt hurt when my teacher called me a nerd. But it turned out to be such a gift to me. I didn't know I could be creative. I didn't know I had it in me. **I didn't get to be creative until I started to create.** And his comment was the trigger that got me started creating.

Appreciate any positive comments from others, too. These little encouragements fuel and boost your confidence in pursuing your passion, especially when you aren't getting support from your loved ones. The compliments I received from Teacher Muzi encouraged me to write more songs and further my skills in music. His belief in me increased my belief in myself, and I'm very thankful for that.

Collect and remember all the compliments you receive. Refer to them when times get tough.

3. Passion is obvious.

It's easy to tell if you are passionate about something or not. When you try it out, you will know if you love it or not. It's pretty obvious.

- Your tone changes when you speak.
- You feel more energetic when you do something you love.
- You want to spend more time doing the thing you love.

That's how I felt when I first started writing lyrics. I was excited to participate in the program. I wasn't just a passive listener.

Ideas to Help You Identify Your Passion

Identifying your passion is important. Not because it will make you rich, successful, or happy. It's because knowing what we love is part of knowing yourself. Self-knowledge is crucial to your personal growth and decision making. If you don't know what you love, how do you create a life that you love? And how do you make decisions that align to what you love?

Here are a few ways to help you identify your passion better.

1. Take Personality Tests

Personality tests are very helpful for starters. I love doing them and did a ton of them when I was planning for my career switch. It helped me understand my preferences and why I behave a certain way. Although they just mostly reaffirmed what I already knew about myself, it did increase the confidence I had in my strengths and helped me understand myself a little more.

Some personality tests provide suggested careers. Do they help you to identify what your passion is? No. None of the personality tests told me to be an animator. It wasn't on the list of suggested careers, but the results did confirm that I love to do creative things. These tests are a good starting point if you aren't confident about what you love. But instead of getting jobs that are suggested by the personality tests, identify a common pattern from the results.

Another thing, the suggested careers relate more to your personality traits and strengths. The test tells you almost nothing about what you love. A few of the personality tests suggested that I should be an accountant. I already knew I was good at organizing and analyzing information, but it was not something I wanted to do for the rest of my life.

Personality strengths don't necessary
relate to passion.

So take note of the top two or three groups of careers that are suggested to you. Don't just look at the top one.

Recommended Personality Tests:

- Myers-Briggs Type Indicator (MBTI)
  http://www.myersbriggs.org/
  My MBTI personality type: INFJ (Introverted, Intuitive, Feeling, Judging)

- Dewey Color System
  http://www.deweycolorsystem.com/
  My best occupational category: Creator
  Second-best occupational category: Organizer

- Dr John Holland's Self-Directed Search (SDS)
  http://www.self-directed-search.com/
  Dr John Holland's test is rather informative. It gives you a summary code of your top-three "types." My summary code is ACS (Artistic–Conventional–Social). I score much higher in Artistic and Conventional than the other four codes available.

Most of my results show that I love both artistic and conventional work. The funny thing is they are opposites: One loves disorder while the other loves order. One is original and the other in traditional. That's why I call myself the "Nerdy

Creator." In the end, I choose to pursue my passion for animation and use my organizing strengths to support what I love instead of the other way round. *Ultimately, it is up to you to decide what you want to do with the results.*

2. Look at Your Childhood

My elder brother, who left a job he disliked, used to ask me what he should do with his life and what was he passionate about. It took him a long time to remember that he loves drawing.

My two brothers and I used to draw a lot when we were kids. We used to hold drawing contests and pin our artworks on the wall. It was fun growing up in such a creative environment. But as we grew up, we were so caught up with our studies, our careers, and making money that we forgot what we used to love.

*We humans are so caught up with survival
that we forget what it is like to live.*

To reconnect with your passion, look at your childhood. When you were children, you didn't have to worry about surviving. Your parents took care of that. Other than homework, most of your time was spent doing what you love. So one of the best places to rediscover what you love to do is looking back to your childhood.

Ask yourself these questions:
- What did I love to do as a child?

- What were my hobbies in the past?
- What did I usually do after school?
- What activities did I enjoy doing in school, during recess, or as extracurricular activities?
- What was my favorite subject in school? Why did I like it?
- Do I still enjoy these activities now?

3. Look at Your Inspirations

Sometimes, if you have no clue at all, you can look externally for inspiration. Most of the time, passion begins with inspiration. You must have seen something or someone do something that makes you want to do the same. The inspiration can also come from movies, TV shows, or articles in magazines and newspapers where they give you glimpses of what kind of work is involved in some occupations.

Look around you and ask yourself:

- Who has inspired me?
- What has inspired me?
- Why do I feel so inspired by that person or thing?
- Who have I met or seen on TV who makes me go, "Oh, I want to be like him or her?"
- Who do I look to as a role model or idol?
- What have I seen people do that I am interested in trying?

A word of caution: Sometimes, people mistake what their role model does as their passion. They may look at a singer they adore and think that they love singing. Therefore, be sure to ask yourself the following questions:

- Have you sung before?
- Do you really love singing or just the applause and recognition that a singer receives?
- Are you just inspired by the charisma and the confidence that a singer has on stage?

You can receive the same recognition from doing something else other than singing. It could be acting, dancing, or something else that is totally not related to the performing arts. You need to discern precisely what you love about your inspiration. Is it their personality or the things they do?

4. Look at Things that Drive You Crazy

As passion evokes strong emotions and energy, so do things that drive you crazy. You can find your passion by looking at things that you hate instead.

For example, if bullying drives you crazy, or if you have been bullied before, your passion might be to stop bullying in this world. You can start a cause or open an organization to help people who are bullied. Or, if you hate your job because it's too manual, your passion might be to simplify and automate work processes. You can set up a company to help other companies simplify and automate their work processes.

Ask yourself the following questions:

- What are the things that drive me crazy?
- What are things that I absolutely cannot stand?
- What makes me sad?
- What are the things that irk me that I want to improve?
- What can I do to stop or minimize these things?
- What are some causes that I feel like contributing to?

Passion does not have to be associated with a job. By looking at the things that drive you crazy, you can easily find a cause to be passionate about or an organization to do volunteer work for. Read the opening story in chapter 12 about Dr Siew, an aesthetic doctor who has a passion for saving dogs. Seeing street dogs put to sleep upset him, so he started rescuing them.

Here are some other examples:

Things that drive you crazy	Your passion might be to...	What can you do?
Drinking and driving	Discourage drinking and driving	Volunteer at organizations like MADD (Mother Against Drunk Driving) to educate the public on the dangers of drink and drive

Seeing people who are poor	Help people who are poor	Set up an organization like CARE to fight poverty
Seeing people do work that they do not care for	Encourage people to pursue their passion	Write a book to inspire people to take action on their passion (like me!)

5. Look at What You Are Interested In

I'll explain the differences between passion and interest later in this chapter, but one thing to note first is **interest is not passion.**

People get confused between the two. They are actually quite different. However, what you're interested in does give you some idea of what your passion is and sometimes it can be developed into your passion. So don't rule it out.

Ask yourself the following questions:
- What do I want to know more about?
- What activities do I want to learn how to do?
- Which of my interests do I want to explore further?
- What courses do I feel most like taking for my own interests?
- What type of books am I most interested in reading?
- What types of TV programs or movies do I love to watch?

6. Ask Your Friends and Family

You get excited talking about the things you love. That's a good clue to identifying your passion. But sometimes, you get too engrossed in the topic you love or the one you thought everyone shared the same enthusiasm about as you, only to find you're the only one excited about it.

Get your friends and family to help you on this. But instead of asking them questions like what they think you love to do or what your passions are, ask them how you react to certain topics. Their replies will be more useful and informative.

Ask them the following questions:

- What topics do I love to talk about?
- What topics cause my face to light up when I talk about them?
- What topics do you feel I can talk about forever without stopping?
- What topics do I appear the most interested in listening to?
- What topics do I have more enthusiasm for than the people around me?

7. Ask Yourself

Identifying your passion is all about asking questions. Most of the questions above are directed at yourself. **You know what you love to do.** You have the answers. You just need to dig a little further to be conscious of them. The best way to identify your passion is to ask yourself.

Nobody knows you better than you.

As long as you are honest with yourself and not filter your answers to the questions, you will find out what you love to do eventually.

Here are a few more questions you can ask yourself:

- What do I love to do if I have the time?
- What excites me?
- What gives me energy when I do it?
- What have I dreamt about doing?
- What would I do for free?

Write Down Anything that Feels Like Passion

Your thoughts come and go fast. Once they are gone, they are gone. So, capture all the inspiration you receive on a piece of paper. Just write down anything you feel or think might be your passion. Get them out of your mind and onto something tangible first. Then, investigate later.

Visualizing your passion in your mind and looking at it written on a piece of paper are different. Looking at it on paper can give you new perspectives. Occasionally taking out your paper and looking at what you wrote with fresh eyes might trigger new ideas and inspire you to act on your passion.

Don't limit yourself to career passions. Explore what you love to do outside work. It can be your hobbies. It can even be activities like chatting with your friends or playing with your children. Your passion doesn't have to bring you any money. What's important is to lay everything you love out first and see how they can link with each other.

Be Honest with Yourself

How accurately you can identify your passion depends on how honest you are with yourself when answering the questions. Don't filter away what you love to do because you are afraid of being laughed at or making mistakes. You cannot pursue what you love when you keep filtering your love away. Be honest with what you love to do and give it the attention that it deserves.

Exercise #1: My Top-Five Passion Wannabes

The purpose of this exercise is to brainstorm about what your passion might be. Treat all the things you write down as possibilities aspiring to be your passion. There's no need to commit to any of them just yet.

1. Revisit the different ways you can identify your passion in the previous section.

2. Write down your responses to the suggested questions. Just write down anything that comes to mind. Don't filter anything out, even if the responses don't make any sense right now or

> sound ridiculous and impossible to you. You don't have to show the paper to anyone.
>
> 3.   After answering the question, circle the five responses that you love the most, excite you the most, and give you the most energy. They will form your top-five passion "wannabes," which you are going to explore further.

How Do You Know If Your Passion Is Real?

First, I want to clear up a couple of misconceptions that people have with regards to what passion is.

Misconception #1: Interest is Passion

People often mix up passion with interest. I once read someone's post online who argued how following your passion will not serve you if your passion is "watching YouTube videos." I'm not sure how much anyone loves to watch YouTube videos, but let's take this as an example.

Let's investigate what makes "watching YouTube videos" an interest or a passion.

Passion	Interest
is what you love to do	is what you like to do
has energy	has no energy
tells me something about you	does not tell me anything about you
has purpose	has no purpose
evolves	changes

When you have passion, you are more likely to...	When you have interest, you are more likely to...
be participatory	be passive
commit to long-term goals	have a short attention span

Figure 7.1 The main differences between passion and interest.

- **Is it something you love to do or just something you like to do?** Love is stronger than like. There are strong emotions when it comes to love. If your passion is indeed watching YouTube videos, you will feel an emotional connection with it. You will feel something about it.

- **Do you feel a sense of energy?** If you don't jump out of your bed every morning feeling excited about watching YouTube videos, then probably it's not your passion. If you are passionate about something, you will have the energy and desire to do more of it. It's unlikely for someone to get excited from watching videos unless it's your favorite TV program. Like for me, I only get excited prior to watching *Survivor*. The show brings me energy.

- **Does it say anything about you?** Interest doesn't tell me anything about you, other than you watch a lot of YouTube videos. It doesn't tell me what you love to do and why you are watching so many videos. If you watch videos to see how the information is presented, then it's more likely to be your passion. From that reason, I know something about you. I know you care about how information is presented visually through video.

- **Do you have a sense of purpose?** Unlike passion, interest does not have purpose to it. If you are watching videos one after another without a purpose in mind, that's probably not your passion. You are just wandering around sites and filling up your time. You can watch the video or not; it doesn't really matter to you. But if you watch videos with the intention of learning how others make their videos, then you probably have a passion for making your own videos.

- **Are you participating or being passive?** When you are passionate about watching something, you will have extra energy that you want to dissipate. Fans of TV shows participate by blogging about the show they love or sharing their thoughts in a forum. There must be some other actions you feel like taking after watching it. If you just play a passive role in watching the videos, most likely it's just an interest.

- **Are you committed to it?** If you are passionate about doing something, you're more likely to form goals or schedule around it. For example, if you are a fan of a show, you will watch the show every single week without missing an episode. If you do not set aside time each week or day to watch YouTube videos, then that is not a passion.

- **Does it stay for long?** Passion that dies off easily is not your real passion. Interest changes all the time. Those things out there that catch your attention or distract you for the moment are not your passions. People have the misconception that passion will change, but it does not! The importance and energy level can vary, but passions don't die—they only evolve. For example, my passion in animation evolves from watching animation to making animation.

Though interest is not passion, it has the potential to become one if you explore it further.

Misconception #2: Passion Is the Thing or Subject Matter You Love

Sometimes, people see the things they love as passion. For example, some people say their passion is dogs, or food, or sports, and so on. There is nothing wrong with loving things.

But passion is about **doing** the thing you love, not just the thing itself. Let's take sports for an example. Sports, itself cannot be a passion because it doesn't tell me anything about you. It doesn't tell me what you love to do with sports. You must be part of the equation when it comes to defining passion.

So if you love sports, ask yourself:

- What do I love about sports?
- What types of sports do I love?
- Do I love to play sports?
- Is there a particular sport I love to play?
- Do I love to watch others play sports?
- Why do I love to watch sports? Is it because the particular sport interests me, or is it because I love to watch competition between two opposing teams?

All of the above questions are somewhat different. Be clear about your answers. Having a passion for watching sports does not mean that you have a passion for playing sports. Asking yourself questions like these in the examples sets you thinking on why you love the things you love and what are you going to do about them.

You Have to Do It to Know It

Exploring your passion is somewhat like dating. In dating, you do not know if you are compatible with someone until you have dated him or her. Same goes with passion. You do not know if your passion is really your passion until you explore further.

As in my case, I created three blogs before I settled on my current one (nerdycreator.com). I love writing, but I don't have the passion to write on every subject that I know or love. It takes time to find the voice in my writing and the thing I am really passionate writing about. And I won't know until I explore and try it out.

Merely loving something does not produce any result.

It is just a fantasy in your head. In dating terms, it is called a "crush." You can't say your passion is playing the guitar when you haven't even played a guitar before. Watching others playing the guitar and loving it does not count! For all you know, you might pick up a guitar and absolutely hate it. Don't just assume your passion is really your passion. It's not advisable to quit your day job and get into something that you have never tried before.

If you are unsure you have passion for something or not, the easiest way to know is simply by doing it and getting feedback. If you are passionate about something, you will feel happy, energetic, and motivated doing it. You can do as many tests or answer as many questions as you want to find what your passion is, but if you don't try it out, you will never know.

Exercise #2: Audition Your Passion Wannabes

Passion needs to be explored. Let all your passion wannabes go through an audition process. Not all the wannabes have what it takes to be your passion.

1. First, go through your top-five passion wannabes list in Exercise #1. If any of them are things or subject matters like sports, technology, health care, and so on, rephrase them so they are activities that you can do.

    Example:
    Instead of saying your passion is hockey, say your passion is playing hockey. Instead of saying your passion is health care, say your passion is helping others to be healthy.

    If you are unsure what you love to do about the thing you love, it's okay; just pick one activity first.

2. Decide the order to audition your passion wannabes. You can pick the one you are most excited about as the first one. It doesn't matter because you are going to audition all of them anyway. Just get them in order: 1, 2, 3, 4, 5.

3. Spend one whole week on passion wannabe #1. Allocate

time after work and during the weekends to read more about your passion via online or in books. Watch videos of people doing your passion. Just gather all the information you can find.

4. At the end of the week, assess how interested you are to explore it further. You can visualize yourself doing it and write down how it feels like, looks like, or sounds like. Give it a rating 1 (being not at all interested) to 10 (extremely interested). Make notes of what you like about it and not like about it.

5. Continue with passion wannabe #2 and so on with Steps #3 and #4.

6. After you have assessed all five passion wannabes, choose one to be the passion you want to explore further.

7. Spend three months on your chosen passion. Find out if there is any course you can take or any organization you can join. Make sure you get to *do* your chosen passion.

8. After three months, reassess if you are passionate about it. Consult your heart on this.
   o If yes, ask yourself what you love about it and continue with your passion.
   o If no, understand why, too. What parts of your passion do you like and not like? If you think your passion is too challenging, it might be a sign of fear. Maybe you want to investigate further and give it another shot.

9. If you really don't like it, pick the next, best passion wannabe to be your passion and revisit Step #7.

Convince Yourself to Listen to Your Heart

Passion comes from your heart. I know how difficult it is to listen to your heart sometimes, especially if you are a thinker. Every time you want to do something, your mind messes with you by telling you why you should not do it instead. I've gone through numerous battles in decision making myself. Being a feeling type of person with a very talkative mind, I have learned to trick myself to accept what I love.

Here's an example of how I do it.

One day, I was sitting on the steps of TKTS Times Square, deciding what to watch in the evening. I wanted to watch the play *Orphans* starring Alex Baldwin, Ben Foster, and Tom Sturridge, but I had such a hard time because my mind kept telling me I should watch a musical instead.

My mind just babbled nonstop:

- Don't watch *Orphans*. It's a play. You aren't good in English. You won't be able to comprehend it.
- Watch a musical instead; at least you can enjoy the music. Don't waste your money and your time. You won't enjoy it. You will regret it!
- *Orphans* is a drama. It's too serious. You won't have fun watching it. Watch something much more lighthearted, like *Nice Work If You Can Get It* instead.

I sat there for the next half an hour in the cold, miserable, and couldn't make up my mind. Instinctively, I knew my heart wanted to watch *Orphans*, but my mind just refused to give way. So, I decided to beat my mind at its own game. *I decided to convince my mind to watch Orphans intellectually.*

I came up with the following reasons to convince my mind:

- I had not watched a play during my entire trip to the United States. Watching a play will add a different aspect to what I've experienced with the other musicals I've watched so far.
- *Orphans* is much shorter. I can join my friends for the night activities earlier.
- *Orphans* starred Hollywood actors like Alec Baldwin. It will be cool to watch him act in person.
- According to the website synopsis, there's some comedy in the drama. It should be well-balanced and entertaining.

In the end, with all these reasons, my mind was sold.

Your mind is very good at many things, like analyzing and organizing, but when it comes to knowing what you truly desire, it's absolutely bad at it. Don't let it dictate what you love. Convince it to accept what you love instead.

Exercise #3: The Passion-Detector Test

A passion-detector test is like a lie-detector test: the purpose is to detect how authentic your passion is. Sometimes, your mind tricks you into believing you love to do something when you actually don't.

Below are questions that you can ask yourself to check if your passion is real or not. Answer either "yes" or "no."

- Do you give up your passion easily when a challenge or an obstacle appears?
- Is your current passion a replacement for another passion you have not tried?
- Do you feel something missing from your passion, like something isn't quite right?
- Does your passion feel too safe, too logical, and perhaps too boring to you?
- Are you pursuing your current passion in order to get something else you want?
- Do you feel like it is a chore to pursue your passion?
- Do you wonder when your passion will end?
- Do you pursue your current passion only because you think you can do it?
- Will you give up on your passion if you know you cannot monetize it?
- Do you need constant discipline and external motivation to pursue your passion?
- Are you always thinking about other things when you are pursuing your passion?

If you answer yes to any of the question above, you might have a fake passion, or it could be that fear is obstructing your progress. Investigate further.

Chapter 8

WHAT TO DO WHEN YOU HAVE MANY PASSIONS

TAJUAN "TEEJ" MERCER HAS NO IDEA that her twenty-year experience and passion as a television editor would eventually make her a reality TV coach. She even resisted it at first, because she was so afraid of what her colleagues might think of her.

TeeJ always knew she wanted to be in the television industry, but she wasn't sure how. After graduating from Howard University in Washington DC, she interned at a television station in Los Angeles to get some inspiration. During her internship, she met a television editor who showed her what an editor does at work. After her explanations, TeeJ knew instantly she wanted to be an editor.

Editing gave TeeJ creative control. She loved that she was the last person to touch the television program before it went on air to the viewing audience. She didn't like working on the set, as there were too many variables beyond her control. She needed to be in control and editing provided that. *She was a control freak!*

For twenty years, TeeJ was happy and comfortable with her editing career, until one day when several people suggested she should be a reality TV coach.

Value Is Relative to People

TeeJ was in a business-coaching program, and her classmates constantly asked her for tips on how to create better videos for their websites. She wanted to write a guide for them, but then she had a better idea. Why not write a book to teach people how to get on their favorite reality show? And before she knew it, people were telling her she should coach people, too and get paid for it.

However, TeeJ doubted it.

Although she had experience with editing reality shows, why would anyone be willing to pay her to be their reality TV coach? What would her editing colleagues think of her? *"Who does she think she is to coach people to get on a show?"*

Furthermore, TeeJ felt that if anyone were going to spend money on her, she had to guarantee them something. But she wasn't a casting director. She couldn't guarantee that anyone would be on a reality show. It was difficult for her to reconcile what she thought a coach should provide with what she could offer as a television editor. She wasn't sure she could offer any value to reality show hopefuls.

It was not until one of her coaches tricked her into believing she could offer something valuable to others that she started believing it was possible.

One day, TeeJ's coach called her and said, "I want to be on a reality TV show. I've made it to the next round of the callback, what do you think I should do?" Since TeeJ has tons of experience in storytelling as a television editor, she knows what makes a great story. Plus, some of her friends are the biggest casting directors in the reality show arena. Giving advice on how to get on reality shows is easy for her. So, for half an hour, TeeJ just kept telling her coach what she had to do to get on the show she wanted.

At the end of the call, her coach shocked her by saying,

"You do realize you just completed your first coaching call."

"No, I didn't," TeeJ replied.

All TeeJ thought she was doing was helping her coach. She didn't realize that after two decades in the TV industry, she knew way more than an average person does. Although she might not be able to guarantee her clients a spot on TV, she could help them prepare, understand what directors are looking for, and get way closer to achieving their goal. And that is very valuable to many other people.

TeeJ still had doubts about her new title, but she went ahead with it anyway. After one of her clients landed a spot on a reality show, she fully embraced her new role. Now, she wouldn't trade it for anything else and can't imagine not doing this job.

Key Lessons from TeeJ's Story

1. Don't hold onto your identity too tightly.

TeeJ was a television editor for a long time. When it was time to let go of her passion and let it evolve into something better, she held onto it tightly. She didn't believe she could provide value as a reality TV coach because she was limited by what she thought a television editor could or could not do. **It was safe to be familiar.**

Prior to being a reality TV coach, TeeJ had a similar experience. She wrote a book called *40 Days Till 40RTY*, which she had no intention of writing. She only wrote it because it was God-inspired. Initially, she didn't even believe she could do it because she thought her storytelling strength was in videos, not in writing. However, in the end, she wrote the book in a week and it went on to receive three Beverly Hills Book Awards.

Holding tight to your current professional identity doesn't allow your passion to grow to its full potential. You must be willing to give up your identity and move on to another role when the time comes.

You have to let go to receive.

TeeJ shared that at some point, a trapeze performer has to let go of the rope he is holding and grab the other rope for the performance to be magnificent. Fear is in the space between the rope you are holding and the other rope. You have to let go to get to the other side.

2. Being fearless comes with experience.

You can never overcome fear completely. Absence of fear is not realistic. You just have to take a leap of faith, try something new, and get over the uncomfortable phase.

You will fear less as you take more action. When TeeJ first starting editing, she was so afraid to take jobs that she didn't have experience in. Fast forward ten to fifteen years into her career, she had no fear anymore. She wasn't nervous about editing new genres of shows. But when she decided to write a book or be a reality TV coach, her fear came back again. She was afraid because they were something new that she had no experience in. However, **fears aren't necessarily the truth.**

TeeJ was afraid that others would think negatively about her if she were to be a reality TV coach. But after she became one, instead of getting criticized, she received positive messages from her colleagues saying how proud they were of what she was doing. They felt she was courageous to take her editing career and build another career out of it. All the fears she experienced were for nothing.

Don't let your fear hold you back from taking action. For all you know, there is nothing to be afraid of.

3. You don't have to choose between two passions.

TeeJ loves editing and helping people. But initially she was torn about the reality TV coach idea. She wanted to separate the two.

She didn't want to mix her passion for television with coaching. She wanted to be a coach who teaches resilience and touches humanity, not someone who lands other people on a television show. It felt shallow to her.

Later, TeeJ realized she need not separate the two; both are part of who she is. When her clients connect with her, they end up learning resilience, too. Once she became aware there is a higher mission to what she does, it was easier for her to incorporate the two. And now she even has a slogan for her two passions: "Resilience is my reality."

Having Many Passions Makes You Unique

Having many passions is definitely a blessing, but it can also be a curse if you are overwhelmed by them. If you want to master your craft, you need to focus. But to focus doesn't mean that you should choose one passion and give up the rest. Here's why.

Less Is More, but More Is Niche

Information is readily available today. It's very easy for people to pick up new knowledge in many different disciplines. It's a disadvantage to only specialize in one area. How are you going to differentiate yourself from your competitors?

Having more than one passion makes you special and helps you develop a niche in your market. Let's say you have a passion for web designing and you have a passion for psychology. Instead of designing websites for random customers, you can design websites for psychologists and clinics. You understand what a psychologist needs for a website more than other web designers who have no interest in psychology. It's easier for you to connect with psychologists because you know their language.

Or, maybe you want to find an IT job. If you love finance and have knowledge in it, you can pitch yourself to banks or investment companies. Likewise, someone who has a passion for electronics can pitch herself to companies that create electronics products. That will increase her chances of being hired.

Combine and Create New Passions

When you have too many passions, combine them and create new ones. Then you can pursue two or more passions at the same time without worrying about choosing one to pursue.

In chapter 7, I explain why you shouldn't just define your passion as a thing or a subject matter. You need to know what you love to do about it. One reason is breaking your passion down into actions and subject matters helps to create new passions. You can mix the different actions and subject matters and have fun testing them out.

Let's say you have several passions below. How can you combine your passions?

Passion (Actions based)	Subject matter
- love solving complex problems - love figuring out how things work - love building things	Engineering
- love conserving energy - love protecting nature - love growing plants	Environment
- love reading finance news - love investing	Business
- love playing team sports like soccer, basketball - love watching sports games	Sports

1. **Combine subject matter with subject matter**
   - Be an environmental engineer.

- Start up an engineering business that builds products that are environmentally friendly.
- Be a product engineer who designs scoreboards for sports events.

2. **Mix different subject matters with actions**
   - Take part in a team sport or charity event that raises money to protect the environment.
   - Read financial news in the engineering industry and invest in engineering stocks.
   - Educate yourself about the ecosystem and build a product that helps the ecosystem.

3. **Mix actions with actions**
   - Think how you can conserve energy by solving the problem of increasing energy demand.
   - Be part of a team or community that grows plants all over the country.
   - Read books on problem solving.

There are many different ways you can play around with your passions. Write down three to five passions and see what new passions you can come up with.

Combine Your Passions with Other People

If you find it difficult to combine your passions together, try combining your passions with other people. Collaboration makes your life easier. You don't have to do everything on your own, but yet you can create something awesome. All you need to do is to focus on your part and learn how to work as a team.

To start, find similar subject matters or actions. Then, write down everybody's passions and figure out how to collaborate.

For example:

Common Subject Matters	Cars
Passions:	• You love to fix things. • One friend loves to design. • One friend loves to sell and market products. • One friend loves to organize and do accounts.
How can you combine the passions?	Set up an automobile company and each of you contributes to the areas you love.

Common Actions	Taking photos
Passions:	• You love to take black-and-white photos. • One friend loves to take photos of landscapes. • One friend loves to take portrait photos. • One friend loves to take photos of food.

	• One friend loves to take photos of houses and buildings.
How can you combine the passions?	Travel together and create a travel photo book. The book will encompass different parts of your holiday destination.

Be Open to All Possibilities

At first, some of your ideas might sound ridiculous when you combine your passions, but stay open to them. Gather more information on your passions. The more knowledge you have about your passions, the better you can combine them together or with others. Don't limit what your passions can do.

For example, like drawing, don't think that all you can draw is a certain style. Try other styles. Or try designing or painting instead. Try something that is closely related to your passion and mix it up.

Inspiration always surrounds us. An unexpected new event in your life might make you see your passions in another light and give you new ideas. So be open to all possibilities and take action appropriately when inspired.

What to Do with Each Passion?

Having a clear intention is important. You don't hop in a taxi and say you want to go to West Street and expect the driver to drive you along West Street. Instead, you tell the driver the exact address of your destination. The same applies when you are pursuing your passion. You need to be specific with what you intend to do for each passion. It helps you prioritize your passions and plan them.

> **To be clear on your intention, ask yourself the following questions for each passion:**
> - What do I want to do with this passion?
> - Do I want to treat this passion as a hobby or a career?
> - How much time do I want to spend on this passion?
> - What do I hope to achieve from this passion?
> - Why do I want to pursue this passion?

The last question is the most helpful. Asking yourself why helps you understand your motivation. If your "why" is strong, you will be very motivated to take action. It also helps you recognize any actions or ideas that are not align with your intention.

For example, in my case, I pursue animation as a career because I intend to entertain, inspire, and connect with audiences via this medium. When my friends suggested I could earn more money making animation for weddings, I was hesitant. It's not that I'm against money. It just doesn't align with why I pursue animation in the first place. I don't get that kind of connection I'm seeking by doing wedding animation. And if my main intention is to make money, I could have stayed in accounting. Why go through all the trouble of a career switch?

Decide Between Career and Hobby

Not all passions are created equal.

Some passions are more suited as careers, while others are more suited as hobbies. There's no need to pursue any of your passions as a career. You can experience as much joy when you pursue your passion as a hobby.

If you love to sing, you will enjoy it no matter what you do with it. You can sing on a stage, sing in your bathroom, sing in the church, or sing in a karaoke room—it doesn't matter. You don't have to be a singer or a recording artist or sell many records to enjoy singing. The act of doing what you love is already worth the price of admission.

To determine if your passion should be your career, ask yourself these questions:

1. Do I really need a career to achieve what I want?

I choose to pursue animation as a career because I want to animate feature films one day. I want to see my work on the big screen. I want to inspire as many people as I can with my animation. If I pursue it as a hobby, I won't be able to do that.

On the contrary, I never see songwriting as my career because my intention is just to express my creativity and emotions through music. Yes, I want to share my music with others. But I can write music by myself. I don't have to collaborate with others if I don't want to. For animation, I can't. It's a team effort. I can't make a feature film on my own.

So, ask yourself if you need a lot of support from other people to do what you love. You can still collaborate with others even if it's just a hobby, but the commitment level and time contributed by your team member might be much lower compared to a job setting.

2. Am I willing to be a service provider?

Having a passion as a career is definitely more challenging and demanding because you are a service provider. Whether the other party pays you or not depends on how well your service is able to meet your client's needs.

You might need to do something you don't like. For example, if you're an artist and your client is not receptive to your ideas and chooses something dull and unimpressive (in your opinion), you still have to accept your client's decisions. You have to draw something that does not inspire you or else forgo the money.

You might also need to work long hours to meet deadlines. So, are you willing to put stress on your passion? Are you willing to spend most of your day doing this?

3. Am I able to support myself?

The basic requirement of a job is to be able to support oneself. If your passion can't support your living yet, start small first. Make some money from your current job while starting something else on the side. Or perhaps change your current, full-time job to something part-time first. It gives you some money to support yourself and more time to pursue your passion.

How much money you are willing to trade to do what you love depends on the individual. Some people like me don't mind a simple lifestyle, while others need a more luxurious one. **Ultimately, it is what you value.**

I value meaningful work more than eating at expensive restaurants. I value time more than money. I value growth more than stability.

So what do you value?

Concentrate on One Passion at Any Time

When you have many passions, it gets overwhelming to pursue all of them at the same time. I'd tried it before and it was a recipe for disaster.

After I left my job as an accountant, I thought to myself: "Since I'm not working now, I finally can do everything I always wanted to do."

So I squeezed everything I love to do in a single day. I would do my animation, write my blog, play my keyboard, write my song, exercise, sing, create my website, meditate, listen to podcasts, read a book, and more. I crammed so many things into one day, it's not even funny. It doesn't take a genius to figure out what happened next.

I felt stressed; I felt tired; I felt disorientated. I almost had a breakdown.

How did I get to this state? Where did all my time go?

Your passions make you feel like a superhero.
But even superheroes can only
save one person at a time.

No matter how passionate you are, you can only give your full attention to one passion at a time. It's not efficient to do something different every single hour because it takes time to warm up to a new activity. After I realized I messed up my schedule, I start striking things out from my to-do list.

Passion needs to be given enough attention for it to grow. When you have multiple passions, you need to decide which passion to pursue first and give it the attention it deserves.

But that brings us to another problem: what do I pursue first?

Which Passion to Pursue First?

A typical scene in an action-type movie shows the hero faced with a pressing decision to make: "Who should I save first? The lady in distress or the world?"

Although this "superhero's dilemma" is such a cliché, it works because everyone has it. How am I going to spend my time? What should I do first? Spending time on something means not doing something else. You have to make a choice.

There are several ways you can do so. Start by making a list of passions you want to pursue, and then use one or more methods below:

1. Elimination

Go through the list and eliminate those passions that contribute the least to what you want in life. Keep going through the list until you are left with one to three passions. Alternating between two main passions is just nice for me. Having more than three passions at any time can spread you too thin, especially if all of them require a lot of your time.

Elimination means striking some of your passions out from the list and putting them aside. It doesn't mean you throw them away. After you have completed what you set to achieve, let that passion take a break and revive the other passions you have previously eliminated. Rotate your passions.

2. Paired comparison

Paired comparison means comparing two passions side by side and choosing the better of the two. There are a couple ways of doing this.

The first way is the playoff method. Draw a grid with your passions on the top row and in the left column. Then, block off half of the matrix in grey. Next, start comparing two passions at one time (e.g., A with B, then A with C, and so on) and select the one you prefer more. For each comparison, rate how strongly you feel about your preference:

1 = not much; 2 = moderate prefer; 3 = strongly prefer

Example:

Passion	A	B	C	D
A		B, 1	A, 2	D, 1
B			B, 3	B, 1
C				D, 3
D				

So, in the example above, if you prefer B slightly more than A, write "B, 1" in the cell where A meets B. You can find out which passion to pursue first by adding up the scores (A = 2, B = 5, C = 0, D = 4). In this example, Passion B is the one to pursue first. If there is a tie between two passions, go back to the cell where you compare them and see which you prefer more.

The second method is used by Janet and Chris Attwood in their book, *The Passion Test*. You take the first two passions on your list and compare them. The winner moves on to compete with the next passion on the list. The passion that survives at the end of your list is your top passion.

3. Ask yourself powerful questions

If you have noticed, there are a lot of questions in this book. Questions are very powerful when seeking clarity about oneself. They are helpful for reflection and I use them all the time. When you are in doubt about which passion to pursue first, ask yourself these questions:

- **Which passion is the most important to me right now?**

The importance of each passion varies over time because what you define as important changes. Your career might be your highest priority right now but as you grow older, family might become more important than your career.

- **Which passion needs the most attention right now?**

Think of a mum who has many kids. She cannot possibly divide her attention equally among all her children. Naturally, she will nurture and give more attention to her newborn child. That doesn't mean that she doesn't love her other children anymore. Same thing when you pursue your passion. Your newer passions need more attention from you and most likely you would prioritize them first.

- **Will I regret not doing this in the future?**

Go through each of your passions and ask yourself this question. If you know in the future you are going to regret not pursuing it now, why not make it a priority and do something about it now?

4. Feel the energy level

This is my favorite way to prioritize passions. If you are more intuitive, try this method instead. At any point, ask yourself to feel:

- Which passion feels the strongest in terms of energy now?

- Which passion gives you the most positive vibe?
- Which passion do you feel most excited pursuing?

Go where your passion energy is the strongest. When you are energetic about something, it's the best time to act on it and get the most work done. I didn't plan to start on this book in 2013 because I was already busy with my animation demo reel. But when I saw an e-mail on this book-writing course, *Bestseller Blueprint*, it reignited my passion for writing. I felt a surge of energy to write, so I went for it. I'm happy that I did because I completed this book in less than a year. Previously, when I tried writing a book when my passion energy for writing was low, I couldn't even get past the first chapter.

Over the years, I have learned to go with my energy flow. If I feel strongly about something right now—like my animation—but I do something else instead, I will feel distracted because my heart is in animation. I'm less efficient even though I am passionate about both activities. The energy level for each passion varies throughout the year, the week, or even the day. Going against the flow of the strongest energy source disrupts the natural flow that passion brings us.

Set Goals to Keep You Inspired

Setting goals gives your passion a place to direct its energy to. It measures the growth of your passion. It's easy to set goals for your passion when you know why you want to pursue it. The key, however, is to set goals that are big enough so that you have the desire and motivation to get there.

There are three ways your passion can play a part in goal setting:

1. Set goals for one particular passion.
    (For e.g., if your passion is marketing, your goal can be to complete your marketing course by 31st Dec 2015.)

2. Set big goals that include one or more of your passions.
    (For e.g., if your passion is marketing and product design, your goal can be to design and sell ten thousand units of your product by 31st Dec 2015.)

3. Set goals that are not related to your passion and see how your passions can help you achieve your goals.
    (For e.g., it can be a financial goal to make $1 million by 31st Dec 2015. Then think of ways your different passions can help you to achieve that goal.)

Managing Big Goals

Setting big goals can be fun and inspiring, but it can also be daunting. The way to manage your big goals is to make them smaller. Start with your ultimate goal and break it down into several milestone goals. Then, break down each milestone goal further into action steps.

*   **Ultimate goal:** It is your destination, your desired end result. It doesn't change unless it doesn't align with your life purpose anymore.
*   **Milestone goal:** This is also what I call the "celebration goal." When you reach this goal, you should take time to

celebrate. This goal marks your success in reaching a significant stage of your ultimate goal.

- **Action steps:** They are small, little steps you plan to take to achieve your milestone goals. How small should the action steps be? As small as they can get. Set them so easy and achievable that you know you can do them and therefore will be inspired to take action on them.

For example:

		Done by:
Intention:	To display my portfolio and let potential clients know of my existence	
Ultimate goal:	Launch my own freelance website	31 Dec 2015
Milestone goals:	#1 - Map out the wireframe for each page	1 Sep 2015
	#2 - Design the first draft of the website	1 Dec 2015
Action steps for Milestone Goal #1:	• Decide how many pages I should have for my website	1 Jul 2015
	• Write out the content for the "About Me" page	1 Aug 2015
	• Write out the content for the "Services" page	7 Aug 2015
Action steps for Milestone Goal #2:	• Gather all my portfolio work in one folder	1 Oct 2015
	• Create the logo for my website	15 Oct 2015

	• Research my competitors	1 Nov
		2015

Deadlines Don't Have to Be Deadly

Imposing deadlines on your action steps and goals keeps you going and accountable. It helps you reach your goals faster as you won't have time to be perfect. **Being perfect slows you down.**

But don't get too stressed over a deadline. A self-imposed deadline is just a check to see how much you have completed at a certain point in time. Sometimes, it's difficult to gauge how much time you will spend doing something. If you can't complete the task on time, just set a new deadline. Assess how you can complete the task faster and continue to work on it. Don't give up because you can't complete it within your self-imposed deadline.

You Need to Complete What You Start

When you have many passions, it is important to complete the tasks you set out for your passions. Don't leave unfinished work aside and start new projects. You can alternate between two or three big projects in a day, but make sure you dedicate 100 percent of your attention to one passion at any point in time. Starting too many new projects at a time is going to leave a lot of projects incomplete. And incomplete projects are going to steal attention from you and distract you.

Completing projects **frees up attention** for other passions. After you complete a task, it's likely that your energy level for that passion drops and you need less attention for it. If that's the case, make it a lower priority and direct your energy to other passions.

Not Completing Is Worse than Not Starting

*You don't want to be
doing everything but completing nothing.*

If you consistently cannot complete what you set out to do, it is time to cut down on the number of your projects and focus, even if it means you are left with only one project.

Not completing you tasks does more harm than not starting at all. It gives you an opportunity to blame yourself. It also erodes your confidence and acts as an excuse to not start new projects in the future. Plus, you are less productive when you don't focus. Every time you switch to a new task, you need to warm up your engine and pick up where you left off again.

Completion gives you positive evidence that you can complete what you set out to do. It increases your self-confidence and trust. Once you complete something, you *know* you can complete it again the next time—it's not merely a belief anymore. You have the experience.

The only time you don't need to complete a project is when you realize it does not serve your purpose anymore and you decide to abandon it for good.

Chapter 9

USE PASSIONS TO BUILD THE SKILLS YOU WANT

I USED TO HAVE LOW SELF-ESTEEM and writing to myself cheers me up. Many people were surprised to hear I was writing a book, but I'm not. I've been writing my whole life. I have written lyrics, poems, short stories, journals, and so on. But I understand why people don't know I love writing. I don't share what I write. For the longest time, I kept my writing private as a way to encourage myself.

Writing helped me through the darkest days. I was extremely quiet in secondary school. A few of my classmates shunned me to avoid having awkward conversations. It was even more depressing to see my classmates fighting not to be paired with me. I couldn't connect with anyone in class. But when I started writing, I felt a connection. I felt like I was writing to a friend.

Here's a short story (parable) I wrote while looking at the beautiful moon one night:

The moon feels sad. Even though the stars are there with him, he feels lonely. The stars joke about his size and his round face. They look down on him because he can only reflect light from the sun.

One night, the stars mock, "Hey, dim moon! The light you're reflecting is not strong enough. Look at the people in the cities. They have to switch on their own lights to see. Their lights are brighter than yours."

The moon cries. He thinks he's very useless. The people don't need him. The stars don't like him because he's different. He doesn't wish to stay here anymore. As each night passes, the moon gets less confident. The less confident he gets, the smaller in size he becomes. Gradually, he diminishes from a circle to a crescent and disappears.

The stars are happy. Now, they can dominate the sky at night. They can get all the attention they want from romantic couples below. But each star has his unique name and wants to be known by the people. So they tried to outshine each other and fight for stardom.

However, most people don't care about the names of the stars. They miss the moon and want him back. The sun feels that the moon should reinstate his position, too. He decides to look for the moon.

When the sun asks the moon to return to the sky, the moon is hesitant. He tells the sun, "You don't work at night. You don't know how mean the stars were. You get to enjoy the vibrant cities. You get to see people work and children play, while I only get to see the people sleep and hear them snore. They need you. They don't need me."

"No, they need you. They love you. They think you are mesmerizing. You see, they don't even want to look at me directly in the eye. Some even find me a nuisance and wear sunglasses and caps to protect against me. But you are different; they admire and look at you," the sun explains. "There is nothing wrong with being different. Both of us are special in our own way. I'll talk to the stars and make sure they don't bully you again. Please come back," the sun reassures and begs.

The moon agrees to return at last and is given a night off every fifteen days. The stars dare not bully him again and later become friends with him. The sun warns them not to mock the moon again, or else they will be banished to the earth as "falling stars."

The moon is happy now. He isn't alone anymore. He believes in himself even though he is different.

***

Writing to myself all those years boosted up my self-esteem. Now that I'm confident, I don't have to write to myself anymore. But then I thought to myself: "If I can write to encourage myself, I can write to encourage others, too." I can put a smile on other people's faces with my writing. So I started sharing my thoughts via blogs and am now writing a book. Passion gives me the confidence to share myself and my stories.

Today, I write to connect with others—something I failed to do when I was in secondary school.

Channeling Passion into Other Areas

Two years ago, if you asked me to sign up for a marketing course, I'd probably think you were nuts. My passion is in creative work like animation, music, and writing. I've no passion for sales or marketing. Why should I study marketing?

Fast forward to today: I'm in this marketing and publicity course by Bill and Steve Harrison called *Quantum Leap*. I understand the importance of sales and marketing in relation to the creative work I do. Why such a change?

It's because I love writing and I want to spread my message. There is no point in writing a book that inspires others to pursue their passion if there are no "others" reading your book. When I found out about the program *Quantum Leap*, I was excited because the program targets first-time authors like me. If I had no passion for writing a book, I would have no business in learning marketing and publicity. Basically, I channeled my passion for writing to marketing.

Some people see passion as a limitation. Once you have identified what you love, you focus on it and block off anything that does not relate to your passion. *I see passion as an opportunity to learn the skills I need.* Even when I don't have much interest in something, I still can be motivated to pick up the skills.

Isn't that great?

Key Lessons from My Story

1. Pursuing passion gives you confidence.
People with low self-esteem focus too much on themselves.

They judge themselves as unworthy or unwanted. And they don't know how to love themselves.

Pursuing passion shifts the focus from the person to the passion. When I started writing, instead of evaluating my self-worth all the time, I directed my attention and energy to my writing. I had less time to think negatively about myself.

Being passionate teaches you how to love.

It brings out your loving nature. When you know how to love what you do, you can direct the same love toward yourself. And that increases your self-esteem.

2. Connecting with others begins with you.

How much other people connect with you depends on how much you share yourself with them. When you share, you find similarities, and that helps you to bond with others. I didn't connect with my classmates in school because I wasn't sharing much. I didn't love myself then, and I wasn't confident enough to tell other people about myself. And that's why I felt distant.

Love yourself first before anything. Connecting with others is simply directing your love from inside to outside. You can connect with others even if you are different. **Differences create interest.** But it's harder to share yourself when you don't really love what's unique about you.

3. Passion can help you develop the skills you need.

Passion is a good motivator to get the skills you need but don't necessarily love. My passion in writing helps me pick up important skills like marketing. And not just that. As I become more passionate, I'm more excited to share what I love, and that improves my communication skills.

It's much easier to acquire and develop skills when you love something. You want to do more of it. But when you have no love for something and you need to acquire the skill, channel the positive energy you have from your passion toward it. It's a better way to acquire the skill compared to forcing yourself to learn something.

Passion Is a Good Starting Point to Acquire Skills You Want

Skills are crucial in the job market. But skills are what *companies* need; what about *your* needs? Don't forget what you heart desires when developing your skills. Develop skills that are aligned to both your passion and what the market requires. Don't forsake your needs just to satisfy what the market wants.

You can acquire any skills you want. But without passion, you don't have a strong enough purpose and motivation to develop your skills. The jobs that pay the best in the market may not be the ones you enjoy doing. Forcing yourself to pick up skills needed for a job you don't enjoy is so much harder than developing skills that you already have the desire to learn.

So, use passion as the starting point to develop your skills. Know what your passions are and see what the market requires. Then, find a way to connect your passion to what the market wants. It's more natural and easier this way.

Use Passion to Be an Expert

No one is born to be an expert,
but everyone can be one if they continue to learn.

I believe in lifelong learning. There are endless things you can learn. If you are open to learning and the information available, whether it is from books, online, people, or any other resource, you will start to accumulate much of the knowledge you need to be an expert.

Passion helps you to learn and become the expert you want to be. When you are passionate about doing something, you get curious, and then you find out more about your passion. You soak up the knowledge you crave. And from my story, you know it's not just in the areas you are passionate in, but also areas related to them. Passion helps to make less interesting topics interesting enough for us to absorb.

Many disciplines are related to each other. As I'm learning animation, I realize I can draw so much on knowledge that I have previously learned in other disciplines.

- **Physics**—Understanding Newton's three laws of motion help to make the characters I animate more believable.
- **Acting**—The knowledge I gain from watching drama series and observing the actors' body language helps me to express the characters' emotions.
- **Cinematography**—The electives I took while I was at university help me in framing my shots.
- **Singing**—In singing, we learn about mouth shapes and that gave me a basic idea for animating lip syncs.

- **Music**—In music, we learn about rhythm and beat that helps in developing the movement beats of a character.
- **Drawing**—It helps in sketching out ideas.
- **Mathematics**—It helps in understanding the graphs in animation software.
- **Spirituality**—When I get stuck in my animation assignment, I learn how to get unstuck.
- **Accounting**—The planning and time management skills I developed in my accounting job help so much in meeting my assignment deadlines.

Pursuing passion is a two-way street. You can use your passion to dabble in other disciplines. Or you can use knowledge and skills from your previous education and experience to help you pursue your passion. Don't see the knowledge you have acquired previously as a waste. Use it to your advantage.

Everyone Needs a Mentor

Being self-motivated and picking up knowledge from books and online materials is great. But an even better way to get the knowledge you desire is to find a mentor. Learning from a mentor provides several advantages over self-learning:

- **Mentors have experience.** They know what works or not based on their past experiences. Self-learning encompasses a lot of trial-and-error on your own.

- **Mentors know the shortcuts that save time.** You don't have to dig through books and online materials to find the relevant information.

- **Mentors identify your mistakes.** When you learn by yourself, sometimes you are not aware when you did something wrong. Mentors, on the other hand, provide you with valuable feedback to improve your work.

- **Mentors help you clarify your concepts.** If you have any doubts about what you are learning, you can ask your mentor directly. You can't do that with books.

- **Mentors have networks.** They have been in the industry much longer. They can help you connect with other people in the industry.

- **Mentors hold you accountable.** When it comes to self-learning, the only person you have to be accountable to is yourself. With a mentor, there is more at stake. You don't want to disappoint your mentor and embarrass yourself for not turning in your work.

- **Mentors push you to your fullest potential.** People tend to let themselves go too easily with excuses and goals that don't stretch them. It is good to have someone who believes you can do something and pushes you at the same time.

- **Mentors let you know how well you are doing.** Especially when you are graded in a formal education setting.

If you want to be successful at something you love, find someone who has already done it before and learn from him or her. It saves you time and money from experimenting yourself. A mentor does not have to be a formal one, like a teacher in a school. You can have an informal mentoring relationship, too. He or she can be your friend, your friend's friends, relative, peer, or someone online. More importantly, find someone who you trust and respect who has done what you want to do. Talk to him or her and ask how he or she does it. See if he or she can give you some advice or pointers.

Exercise #1: Wake Up Your Knowledge

Sometimes, you forget how the knowledge you previously gained applies to your current life. This is just a simple exercise to help you be more aware of the knowledge and skills you have and how they can contribute to your passion.

Begin by writing your passion in the center of the paper and circle it. Surround it by writing down all the knowledge and skills you have previously acquired.

Here are some areas in which you can look for them:

- Your previous education
- Courses you have taken
- Books you have read
- Topics you have researched online
- Your current and previous jobs
- Personal experiences
- Knowledge and skills you learned from your friends
- Places you have traveled to

Figure out how the knowledge or skills have helped you or can help you to pursue your passion. (See Figure 9.1 for an example.)

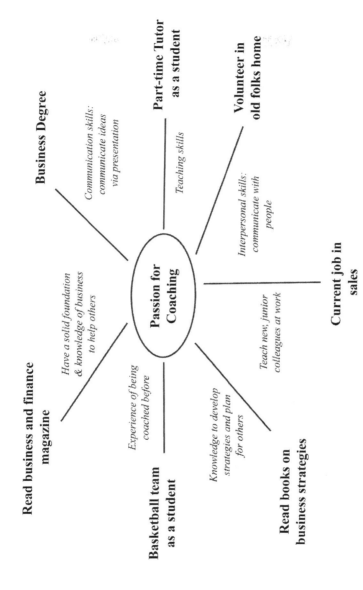

Figure 9.1 A mind map example that shows how your knowledge and skills can contribute to your passion

Use Passion to Increase Your Employability

To fulfill your job and increase your employability, you require more than technical skills. Employers tend to look beyond qualifications and experience when hiring their candidates. They look for soft skills and transferable skills. With passion, you can easily develop these skills and increase your employability.

Ask yourself would you rather:

- Give a presentation on a topic that you are excited about or a presentation on a random topic?
- Write an article on a topic that you are passionate about or a random topic?
- Lead a team in a cause you are passionate about or just lead a team?

When your heart is involved, it is easier to develop these presentation, writing, and leadership skills you need for your job. It's more difficult to acquire skills just for the sake of acquiring them.

The beauty of passion is it makes you forget about the skills you lack and, at the same time, helps you develop them.

Even if you are afraid of public speaking, when you talk about something you have so much passion about you tend to focus more on what you are sharing than your speaking abilities or the audience.

Skills that Increase Your Employability

• Technical skills

Without a doubt, technical skills are the basic requirement to getting a job you love. It is specific to your occupation. You need these skills to perform the daily duties.

(E.g., accountants need to know the accounting standards, how to perform journal entries, etc.)

• Interpersonal skills

Interpersonal skills are your social skills. It is how you relate to other people, like your colleagues, bosses, and customers. Most jobs need people to work together as a team. Employers look for candidates who can fit with their existing team.

(E.g., being tactful, able to work in a group setting, able to build relationships, etc.)

• Communication skills

Communication skills are your ability to express your ideas verbally or in writing, and also how well you listen to others. Good communication skills are required as you advance in your career.

(E.g., giving presentations, negotiating, writing proper e-mails and letters, etc.)

• Computer skills

Computer skills are getting more important as technology replaces manual work and redefines your job responsibilities. You need to adapt to technological changes quickly.

(E.g., able to learn new software quickly, basic IT skills, able to keep up with technological changes, etc.)

- **Organization skills**

Organization skills are your time-management skills and planning skills. It's how well you manage yourself, others, and resources. Time is money. Employers love efficient and productive employees.

(E.g., able to meet deadlines, have an efficient workflow, able to be independent, etc.)

- **Problem-solving skills**

Problems arise unexpectedly every day. Employers look for candidates who can handle stress and solve problems at work. Problem solving can be both analytical and creative.

(E.g., come up with creative solutions, identify, analyze, and resolve issues at work, evaluate the solutions, etc.)

Being passionate about your specialization is the best scenario because technical skill does increase your employability by a large margin. You will want to constantly improve your technical skills. Having a passion in your specialization also easily pushes you to improve other skills over time because you want to do well in your passion.

Partner Up with Your Strengths

Passion and strength are a killer combination. There's no need to argue which is better. Passion provides the energy and strength provides the efficiency. Use your passion to acquire the skills you want and use your strength to speed it up.

For example, let's say you want to improve your planning skills. Your passion is in cycling and your strength is in communicating with others. What you can do is organize cycling outings with your friends. Use your strength in communication by sharing your ideas with your friends and enrolling them to help you with the planning. Get them to organize the event with you and learn from the experience.

It does take a little creativity to connect the dots, but it is fun. If you can't come up with any ideas, ask others for help and suggestions.

Exercise #2: Connect the Dots

This exercise helps you to generate ideas to improve your skills. First, write down at the top the skill you want to develop. Next, list all your passions and strengths in the two columns below. Finally, brainstorm ways to connect your passion and strengths to the skill you want.

Ask yourself:

- How can I use my passion to develop my skill?
- How can I use my strength to develop it faster?

See Figure 9.2 for an example.

Skill that I Want to Acquire:	
Time-Management Skills	
Passions	**Strengths**
• Dancing • Working with numbers • Spending time with my family • Teaching	• Creativity • Communicating with others • Spontaneous • Fast learner

Ideas:

1. Teach a class and practice delivering the material within the allocated one-hour time frame (connect passion with skills).

2. Commit to completing my work at 6 p.m. daily so that I can have dinner with my family (connect passion with skills).

3. Think of creative ways to increase my productivity and improve my workflow (connect strengths with skills).

Figure 9.2 An example to show you how you can connect your passions and strengths to acquire the skill you want.

Chapter 10

HOW TO BRING YOUR PASSION TO WORK

WHEN LEANNE SPENCER FELT SHE WAS LOSING HER PASSION for sales, she decided to start her own business. Leanne had been working in sales at various market-data companies for fourteen years since she graduated. She loves selling. However, as her job was getting more demanding and stressful, it started to affect her well-being, too.

As an account director, Leanne was expected to entertain the clients. She often had to drink heavily and her health was sliding. The market challenges from 2008 onward didn't help, either. It was much harder for her to get new business and her work performance was affected. Feeling rather low about the whole corporate lifestyle and stressed from work for almost two years, she had an epiphany one day in the office: *"Life's too short to do something that makes me unhappy."*

She didn't want to be stuck in the office for another day doing work she didn't like. Sitting around and waiting for things to happen would not change her situation at all. If she wanted a change, she needed to take charge and make it happen herself. So she took a chance and left her job for a career in personal training.

Starting a New Business

Starting a personal-training business wasn't a difficult decision for Leanne. She had a background in sales and she was passionate about running her own business. She wanted to do something that required her to be outdoors, involved health and fitness, and allowed her to change other people's lives. Personal training lets her do just that. Plus, she knew it was something she could start immediately without having to earn a new professional degree.

But starting a new business was not without challenges. Leanne only had a few months of salary in the bank. She paid a £4,000 training fee on credit first. It was risky. What if she didn't have any clients? What if her business didn't work out?

As daunting as her fears were, she knew she had to do it.

Leanne had so much conviction in her vision that it was worth a gamble. Not having much financial support did help motivate Leanne to get more clients, though. She was prepared to do anything to get established. If her client wanted to book a session at 6 a.m., she would do it. If her client wanted to book a session at 10 p.m., she would do that, too. She would accept any hour requested by her clients.

Leanne also put in the effort to do research:

- She contacted successful personal trainers in other areas and asked them for tips and advice.

- She went on the Internet to study different workout exercises.
- When she was in the gym, she would look at the exercises other people were doing.
- She carried on studying online to get more qualifications and keep her skills up-to-date.

Leanne's hard work paid off. She got clients very quickly right from the start through word-of-mouth. And lucky for her, she had a little financial buffer. She managed to sell her house and moved into a much smaller flat during her transition period. Without this move, it would have been much harder.

Not long after, Leanne set up a more specialized company that helps people with anxiety disorders to ease their stress through exercises and massages. She's a lot happier and healthier now with her meaningful, new career, and she saved her passion for sales from dying.

Key Lessons from Leanne's Story

1. Passion needs the right setting to blossom.

Leanne loves sales. But when her passion was applied in two separate contexts, they produced two different outcomes. Her passion for sales didn't work in her previous job because it contradicted her passion for health and fitness. Only when her passion for sales was used in alignment with what she valued in life, was it able to shine.

Sometimes, people don't know why they are unhappy even after they make a career switch to something they love.

It might be because their passion is used in the wrong context. There are other aspects to a job—work culture, salary, the company's location, and so on—that might affect happiness that has nothing to do with what you love to do. Passion is not to be blamed here. Passion can produce good results when it is put to the correct use.

2. You can combine several passions to create what you want.

A career change doesn't mean you have to give up everything and start all over again. Just because Leanne wanted to pursue a career in personal training didn't mean she had to give up her knowledge and love of sales. In fact, she revived her dying passion for sales by combining it with her two other passions—business and fitness. Combining your passions can give you new energy to create what you want.

But you need to believe it's possible first.

Leanne persisted because she believed her business would work. She wanted to bring all three of her passions into her career, and she didn't settle for anything less. And ultimately, she did it.

3. Happiness depends on you.

When Leanne recognized she was unhappy with her job, she did something about it. She knew if she didn't do anything, nothing was going to change for her, and she would remain unhappy at work.

Even though Leanne had not started a business before, that didn't stop her from achieving her happiness. She just leaned into her idea and learned along the way. She kept improving her skills and stayed true to her original intention of helping others. She decided to be happy and worked for her happiness.

Don't let your fears and excuses stop you. If you don't know how to begin, go ask somebody who has already achieved what you want to achieve. It might sound counterintuitive that your competitors would help you. But there are many people out there who love to share how they became successful. Or like Leanne did, ask someone who lives in another area and isn't your direct competition.

No one is responsible for your happiness but you. **If you want to be happy at work, you have to work for your happiness.**

Being Happy at Work Is Your Responsibility

Being happy at work is a necessity, not a luxury. You deserve to do the work you love and be proud of it. Happiness is a choice. If you don't like your job, do something about it:

1. Believe it's possible to do work you love now even if you have no idea how this will happen.

2. Make it a requirement in your life. Commit to it. Don't accept anything less than being happy at work.

3. Be grateful for the things you receive from your current job, for example, salary and friendship. There are always things to be grateful for. If not, you won't be staying in your current job.

4. Find ways in which you can be happier at work, like infusing passion in your current job.

5. Resign and find a job that is a better fit.

6. Create a business that you are passionate about.

Whatever you do, just don't wait for happiness to come. If you're unhappy at work, you have the power to change your circumstances.

Why Do You Work?

Have you ever asked yourself:

*   Why do you work?
*   Why do you need a job?
*   What is the purpose of you current job?
*   Are you currently working for money, to gain experience, or to do the things you love?

Understanding your motivation to work helps you check if your current job is aligned to what you desire. I could have continued to stay on as an accountant, climbed the corporate ladder, and drawn a higher salary if those things are what I wanted to achieve in life. But those things are not what I seek in life. *They are part of someone else's game, not mine.*

Don't play by other people's rules.
Create and play by your own.

I'm happy to sacrifice my salary for meaningful work. I would rather create my own game, play by my own rules, and embrace whatever outcome I face. Good or bad, at least it's my decision. And I blame no one.

Whatever your choice is, be happy with it. There's always something redeeming about your job, such as your salary. People who are unhappy with their jobs often fail to see that they are getting something valuable from the jobs they hate.

Learn to be grateful for what you receive. Know why you work and let it be your motivation to work. If you have other motivations that are important to you, pursue them. Everyone wants different things. Some people want more money. Some people want more freedom and time. Some people want a better working environment. Some people just want to support their families. And sometimes your motivations change as you grow older. Adjust and change your job accordingly.

How to Love Your Job when You Don't

Even if your current job is not something you are passionate about, you can still find opportunities to do what you love. For more than three years as an accountant, though I've no passion for accounting, I wasn't miserable. I was still able to infuse my passions into my work in the following ways:

- **My passion for generating new ideas and problem solving.** I always make the effort and find ways to streamline the work processes and systems on top of my core duties. Not only does it help my work to be more

196 Yong Kang Chan

efficient, I get a chance to infuse my creativity and think of solutions to solve problems.

- **My passion for designing.** As my company changes its operations and has new businesses, I have the chance to redesign the system's user interface and reports. Though it is system designing and not the artistic kind, it's still a form of designing, and I love that.

- **My passion for making others laugh.** I love to laugh and I love to work in a happy environment. It doesn't matter what you do as a living, if you have a passion for entertaining others, you can always find opportunities to tell a joke and bond with your colleagues.

- **My passion for teaching and helping others.** I'm thankful that in my short three years in accounting I was given quite a number of chances to train new employees. Also, I believe in sharing knowledge when it comes to working as a team. So, whenever I discover new methods of doing things, I love to share my knowledge with my other colleagues.

If you are unhappy with your current job, ask yourself: *How do I align my passions with my work?*

Step up and do things you enjoy within or beyond your job scope. Volunteer! Certain passions like entertaining others, teaching, and helping others can be applied to most jobs. Although it might not be part of your core duties, you can always find ways to sprinkle your passions in your job.

Some people might ask why should they do more than what they are being paid for. Truth be told, you don't lose out by going the extra mile. Instead, you gain. When you step up and do things you love, not only will it benefit you, it will also benefit the company and your colleagues. You might also get recognition from your manager for the hard work you put in.

Shape Your Current Job to Be Ideal

Many people don't think it's possible to have an ideal job. There isn't one job that has everything they love to do. The reality is that jobs in the market aren't ideal because the job scopes are created by other people; they are created based on the needs of the company. They have nothing to do with your needs or what you love to do.

*You can't create an ideal job
unless you create one yourself.*

I can already hear some of you moaning right now: "But I don't want to be an entrepreneur!" Well, you don't have to. All you need to do is to take control of your current job.

Have an ideal job in mind and use your passions to slowly shape your current job to as close as what your ideal is. Even if your employer doesn't recognize your passions, talk to your superior and ask if you can do more of the things you love. Give him examples of what you love to do. Communicating with your superior is the key to getting your ideal job.

There will be certain tasks you might not like to do. And you can't get rid of them because you are paid to do them. But try and include more of the activities you love to do into your existing job. **You are the biggest factor in your job satisfaction.**

If you dislike your core duty, change your job. (You will learn how to do this in chapter 11.) If you cannot, why not shift your perspective and accept your job for the time being? Make the best out of the current situation and do your best. You job will not change if you don't do anything about it.

From Employee to Boss

Another way to have an ideal job is to be an entrepreneur. Being an entrepreneur allows you to have more control over your job scope. It gives you more flexibility than working for others. It gives you a lot more freedom to do what you love. You get to delegate or outsource tasks you aren't skilled at or dislike.

The biggest challenge for new entrepreneurs, though is in the beginning they don't have the sales and money to outsource these tasks to others; they have to do many things that they don't have a passion for in order to operate and run their company smoothly.

My brother, who just started an online party, printable business with his friend, told me he felt very stressed and overwhelmed with his new business at times. I explained to him that now he is not only a boss, he is also the finance department, the sales department, the creative department, the legal department, the technical support, and so on. Previously, when he worked in customer service for an established company, all he needed to handle was his own job responsibilities. But now that he is an entrepreneur, he has to be everything that a company needs. He is now part of a two-employee company.

*Not everyone has the passion to be
an entrepreneur.*

Online resources available today are vastly different from just a decade ago. You can do a lot more things now as compared to the past. There are more opportunities for individuals to be entrepreneurs today. But before you decide to create a business from your passion, ask yourself: *Why do I want to have a business in the first place?*

*Don't start a business because you can;
start a business because you want to.*

Having a sustainable business means your business has to be profitable. And being an entrepreneur means you may have to be a leader. Not everyone loves to make profits and lead others. If you are passionate about something, there are other ways to pursue it (as we previously discussed). Creating a business is not the only option available.

Your Ideal Job Might Be Out There without You Realizing

Do you remember the time in school when most of your classmates wanted to be teachers? Children want to be teachers because, other than their own families, they have the most contact with teachers. They never know other jobs exist until these jobs are presented to them.

Even as adults, there are many jobs that you haven't heard about. Most jobseekers consider the more common jobs, like doctor, accountant, and sales rep. They don't think about all the other unusual jobs out there such as:

- Coconut safety engineer
- Flavorist
- Professional sleeper
- Pet food taster
- Nail-polish namer

A job that's unfamiliar to you might be the job that you love. You won't know until you find out more about it.

*Thinking there's no job for your passion
doesn't really mean there isn't.*

It can just mean that you don't know it exists or you are unaware that it's something you love to do. Even if a job is not available in your country, it might be available in other countries. So don't assume there's no ideal job for your passion.

You Are Not Your Job

It's doesn't matter if you are an entrepreneur, fireman, or a police officer. Don't let your job dictate who you are and limit yourself.

You don't need a job title.
You don't need an identity.
You should just be you.

Most people are too attached to their job titles. I always find it amusing that accountants are usually the ones to calculate and split the bills when we dine in groups. Every profession can use a calculator to do simple calculations!

People have beliefs about what a profession can or cannot do. It is as though when you get a job, not only do you get an income, you get all the other labels attached to it—for example, your personality, your strengths, and your identity:

- Accountants are meticulous and good at mathematics.
- Salespeople are extroverts and good at communicating with others.
- Teachers are caring and experts on the topics they teach.

And sometimes, it's not even how others see you—it's how you see yourself. You limit what you can do with your job title. Just because you are a salesperson doesn't mean you have to be glib. Just because you are an accountant doesn't mean you can't be sociable. Even though I was an accountant, I was still creative. And now that I am switching to be an animator, does it mean I suddenly can't count anymore?

Chapter 11

BE PREPARED BEFORE YOU CHANGE CAREERS

WHAT WAS MEANT TO BE A SIX-MONTH, TEMPORARY JOB turned out to be a ten-year career for Anne Rupert because she didn't know what else to pursue as a career.

After graduating from The University of York with a masters degree in English Literature, Anne wanted to save some money to go traveling. She took a temporary position in a large housing organization doing filing and administrative work. However, later she was offered a full-time position, so she continued to work for the company.

Anne was good at her job. In her ten years with the company, she assumed several roles:

- She developed customer service procedures.
- She formulated business plans and made sure that they were delivered.
- She led the company's corporate responsibility agenda.
- She produced the company's annual corporate responsibility report.

Eventually, she was promoted to a managerial role. But there was one problem: *She wasn't enjoying her job even though she was paid well.*

Anne knew for a long time that she wasn't doing something she wanted to do. Although her superiors frequently praised her work, she never felt she achieved anything great. She wasn't proud of her work and didn't have much satisfaction doing something so process-based and routine. *But not knowing what she wanted to do stopped her from leaving.*

Anne didn't know what other careers she could pursue and had no direction or personal goals to work toward. So she stayed in her job for an entire decade, even though she was unhappy.

Planning a Career Break

One evening in July 2013, Anne was having a beer and sitting on the beach with her boyfriend. She was looking at the sea and suddenly she felt rather sad about her life. She felt she had wasted her life doing something she didn't care for. She needed a change. She couldn't let her life just carry on as it was anymore. It was now or never.

Over the next couple of days, Anne decided to do something about her career. She started making plans even though she didn't know what she wanted to do. She had just received a pay raise. She thought to herself that rather than spending that extra money on shoes, she could just save that amount every month until the following spring. With those savings, she could buy herself six months of a career break.

And within the six months, she could do unpaid work and get some inspiration about what she wanted to do next.

Even though Anne had a plan, her fears grew as the resignation date got closer. For her, it was a mixture of fear of the unknown and fear of failure. What if she can't find anything to do during the career break? What if it doesn't work out? And what if this is the wrong thing to do?

But Anne stood by her decision, because she knew *happiness was her priority.* She understood if she stayed in her job, it wouldn't make her any happier. She needed to get herself out of there and explore new things. She was willing to trade her well-paid salary to search for a more meaningful job. Even if her career break didn't work out, she would still have a good experience and broaden her horizons. Most importantly, she could leave her current job.

In April 2014, Anne quit her job, and the week after, she started working as a volunteer with Brighton Festival, England's biggest curated, mixed-arts festival. She had always been passionate about the arts and music and enjoyed attending the festival every year. Although she wasn't an artist, it made her proud to contribute to something she loved. She had a lot of fun playing an active role in the festival.

It might have taken Anne ten years to start exploring her passion, but it was worth it to take that step. From volunteering at the Festival, she expanded her network in the arts industry and that landed her a couple of new projects (both volunteer and paid). From there, Anne will evaluate her experiences and learn more about what she likes and doesn't like in a job before choosing a new career.

Key Lessons from Anne's Story:

1. Don't let uncertainties stop you.

Many times, people stay in jobs they don't like because they don't know what else to do and what their passions are. But the problem with that is they can never get a clearer picture of what their passions are until they start to explore other things outside of their work.

Even after ten years, Anne had no idea what else to do other than her job because her fear of the unknown held her back from exploring other possibilities. She thought it was impossible or difficult to find a better job than what she had.

It was only when she pushed herself out of her comfort zone that she discovered work that was truly meaningful to her. And she wouldn't have known about it if she hadn't taken a career break.

2. Doing meaningful work engages you.

Sometimes, doing what you love is as simple as being part of something you care about. Brighton Festival was something Anne had enjoyed as a customer for the last few years. Being a part of it made her feel proud and excited.

Unlike her previous job where she just went through the motions, she felt great working at the festival because she genuinely cared about it. She could see the impact that the festival and her contribution had on people right away.

And even though Anne's job was challenging, she still felt motivated to contribute. She was a planner at heart, but being a volunteer at a festival forced her to embrace her spontaneous side a little more. She couldn't plan for unexpected events in advance. She had to frequently think on her feet. It was something she felt uncomfortable with and not used to at first, but later she had a lot of fun with the random things that came up, and she started loving being spontaneous.

3. Planning gets you prepared.

You can't plan for everything, but planning gets you started and gives you an overview of what actions to take. It tells you what resources you need to get what you want. **Planning makes uncertainties less scary.**

After Anne decided to leave her job, planning got her thinking about the future and prompted her to answer important questions such as:

- How long will her career break be?
- How much money does she intend to set aside for the career break?
- How much does she need to save each month for her career break?
- When will she be able to reach the amount she intends to save?
- What are some possible jobs she can line up during the career break?

Two years ago, Anne felt it was impossible to take a career break. But after answering these questions, they provided her some comfort to change jobs and an action plan that she could follow. **Planning makes the impossible seem possible.**

A Career Change Needs Proper Planning

Great planning makes passion a viable job option. If you want to change your career, plan your escape route now. Don't wait for your knight in shiny armor to rescue you from corporate hell. Dreaming in your cubicle will not get you a new job. Write down your dream job instead and develop a strategy.

But don't quit your job without proper planning. You might end up in a job that you don't like again or you might be unprepared to give up certain things in the process of switching your career. Here are six questions to ask yourself before you make a career change:

1. Why do you want to quit your current job?
2. Why are you attracted to the new career?
3. Where are the jobs you want?
4. What skills do you need?
5. What are your costs?
6. How much time do you need?

Question #1: Why Do You Want to Quit Your Current Job?

The first stage of planning is to understand what motivates you to quit. The more you understand your motivations, the easier it is for you to decide whether to quit your job.

Ask yourself the following questions:
- Why do I want to quit my current job?
- What is the motivation behind my career change?
- Why do I dislike my current job?
- Why did I stay in my current job for so long?
- Is there anything I like about my current job?
- What are the things I desire that I don't have in my current job?

It's not good enough to know you dislike your job. You must know the specific reasons behind it. Is it certain aspects of the job that you don't like, or is it the career itself you are not passionate about?

There are several reasons why people want to leave their jobs:

- **Bad working environment**
  It can be physical aspects—inaccessible work location, poor office conditions, and slow IT systems—or it can be social aspects—not getting along with bosses, managers, and colleagues. Perhaps the workplace is too political. Or perhaps superiors are not recognizing their efforts or not giving them enough independence to do their work.

- **Stress or no work–life balance**
  Some people quit their jobs because they're too stressful or the jobs are affecting their health. They spend too much time at work and they are given too much work to do. They

want more time for their families, recreational activities, and exercise.

- **Feeling bored at work**
Certain jobs are not challenging enough or too boring. Some employees feel that they are given work that is unimportant and their strengths are underutilized. They want to quit because they want to do much more but aren't given the opportunities in their current jobs.

- **Not content with the current salary**
There might be higher salaries in the job market, or they feel that they are not compensated enough for their efforts.

- **Find no meaning in their work**
They don't believe in the work they do. They don't find their jobs interesting. Their current work doesn't match their values in life and reasons for working. Perhaps they want to add value to other people, but their jobs don't allow them to do so in the way they want.

Not all of the above reasons are good reasons for a career change. If you're unhappy about your working environment, there's no need to change careers. You can just find a similar job in another company. If you love the job but you find it too stressful, think of ways to improve the quality of your work experience. Let your bosses know your problems.

A career change is a wiser choice when you want to do something different or the industry and the nature of the job doesn't interest you anymore. Knowing the exact reasons behind a proposed career switch will help you decide if a change is really necessary.

Question #2: Why Are You Attracted to the New Career?

To justify your career change, you need to have valid *push*-and-*pull factors*.

- *Push factors* are things that make you want to quit.
- *Pull factors* are things that attract you to the new career.

Most people just consider what they hate about their current jobs. They never consider what they like about the career they want to pursue. Having push factors alone doesn't justify a career change. Your new job might not provide you what you love. You might just be jumping from one job you dislike to another job you dislike. And that's going to waste lots of your time and money.

When I was an auditor, I made sure I wrote down all my push-and-pull factors. I didn't just want to find any other job in the market; I wanted to have a job that would bring me closer to what I love doing. I needed some solid reasons to justify my career change before I made the move.

This is what I had written down previously:

Push Factors (i.e., what factors make me want to quit my auditor job)	Pull Factors (i.e., what factors make me want to enter the media and creative industry)
• Find checking and auditing other people's work meaningless and	• Love these industries since I was young. • Many of my passions are

boring.	related to jobs in these industries.
• Don't see the value of doing certain tasks.	
• Have to constantly chase clients for information and documents.	• People in these industries are generally more passionate in what they do.
• Long hours and no time for my passions.	• More opportunities to use my creativity.
• Not enough manpower.	• Casual dress code.
• No fixed working location or desk.	• Fun, happy working environment.
• Most of my colleagues do not like their jobs.	• Love to do project-based work.
• Low morale.	• Feel accomplished to see the end product.

After you list your pull factors, consider how strong they are. Compare them to your current job:

- Are the pull factors similar to what you like about your current job?
- If so, why do you need a career change?
- Can you do an internal transfer in your current workplace instead of leaving?
- Can you negotiate with your boss to make your current job better instead of leaving?
- Are there some pull factors that your current job can *never* provide you?

Do a preliminary check first to see if the things you think about your new career are accurate. Go talk to people who are already in the industry and ask them for their experiences. Also, understand the challenges in the industry so that you are realistically prepared for the future and not overly optimistic about the industry you love.

Exercise #1: Push-and-Pull Factors

Before you make a career switch or quit your job, analyze your push-and-pull factors first. Using Figure 11.1 as a guide:

- Assess and write down what you **like** and **dislike** about your current job.

- Categorize your **likes** and **dislikes** according to the job environment, management, content of the work, and so on.

- Highlight the push factors in the dislike column (i.e., things that you really hate so much that they make you want to quit).

- List all the pull factors of the job you desire.

- Consider if the push and pull factors are strong enough to justify a change in occupation, or is a change in work environment sufficient.

Compare your current job with the job you desire by asking yourself:

- What characteristics attract me to the job I desire that my current job doesn't have?

- Do I think the job I desire has the things I like about my current job?

- If not, am I willing to forsake the things that I like about my current job for the job I desire?

Should I Make a Career Change?		
	Dislikes	**Likes**
Work Environment		
Management		
Content of the work		
	Push Factors	**Pull Factors**

Figure 11.1 A template you can use to decide if you should make a career change or not.

Question #3: Where Are the Jobs You Want?

Once you have decided you want to make a career change, it is time to figure out where you can find your desired job. At this stage, you might not know exactly what the jobs you want to pursue are, but you might have some industries you love in mind.

Start making a list of all the companies in the industry where you think your desired jobs are. Not to worry whether they really do have the job you want or not. To make your list, research online job boards, yellow pages, or simply search in Google. For example, type in "engineering companies in Singapore." In addition to online research, go to networking events and job fairs in your area.

Keep your list simple. Just write down the company name and some of the jobs that interest you. If any particular aspects of a job are very important to you, such as the work location, create columns for them. Include links to the company website so that you can easily refer back to it. You might also want to include links to job openings.

Question #4: What Skills Do You Need?

When you have a list, go through it and see if there are any job openings. Read the job descriptions and see what skills and traits these companies are looking for. Identify the common skills needed. They can be:

- a particular degree or certificate you need to get;
- a particular software you need to know how to use;
- number of years of experience needed;
- soft skills and personality traits; or
- any other things that are required for you to get hired (e.g., a portfolio for designers).

About your desired job, gauge where you are in terms of skills and see what you need to learn to fill in any gaps. Don't get disheartened when your skills don't match up with the job descriptions. Usually things like software, soft skills, and even number of years of experience aren't that big a factor in being hired. As long as you can show in your resume or interview that you can easily pick up these skills or have some related skills and experience in your previous job(s), you should still apply for the position.

The main skills you need to acquire are the ones that are critical to your job. If you are an accountant, you are expected to know how to do accounting. If you are a surgeon, you are expected to know the surgical procedures and how to perform surgery. Understand why your prospective employer needs to hire someone in the first place. There must be some unfulfilled needs in the company, and here is where you come in to offer your help and expertise to the company.

Exercise #2: Transferable Skills

- First, go through the list of companies in the industry you like and write down all the core skills needed for the job you desire.

- Next, write down all your **skills** and **work** you have done for your current job and in school. If you have done chapter 9's "Exercise #1: Wake Up Your Knowledge," you can use it for this exercise, too.

- Compare the two lists and see which skills can be

> **transferable** and **useful** to the job you desire.
>
> - In your resume (and later in your job application), highlight the work you have done that uses these skills.

Question #5: What Are Your Costs?

After you know what skills to acquire, the next stage is to figure out the financial impact this career change will have on you. Find out the following:

- What are your current monthly expenses? What is your current monthly income?
- How much will it cost you to get the skills you need?
- How much money do you currently have saved?
- If you want to quit your current job and pursue your studies, how much money will you need while you are unemployed?
- If you are going to take a salary cut, how much are you willing to sacrifice?

1. Maintain a Budget

It's good to track how much money you spend each month; it tells you how much surplus you have each month. This surplus helps you finance the courses and education necessary for your career change. To calculate your monthly surplus:

Income - Expenses = Surplus

Maintaining a budget might sound like work, but it's not. It can be simple. The easiest way is to deduct your current month's ending bank balance with last month's end amount.

For example:

Month-end bank balance:	
As of 30th Apr 2014	$28,000
Less: As of 31st Mar 2014	($26,000)
Surplus for April	**$ 2,000**

And since you already know what your monthly salary is, you can use it to calculate your expenses for the month.

For example:

Monthly salary	$3,000
Less: Surplus for April	($2,000)
Expenses for April	**$ 1,000**

If you are like me and prefer to know what you spend your money on, track your expenses by category. Break down your expenses line by line in subcategories like food, transport, and insurance. There are also many free apps that you can install to your smart phone that do that. Just develop the habit of entering your expenses into you phone every time you pay for something.

2. Know How Much It Costs to Acquire the Skills

Begin comparing different available courses to acquire your skills. See which course will benefit you the most and what it costs. Consider both online and traditional courses. Choose the best course based on what it teaches, not just on the cost. It must be able to teach you the skills required by your desired job.

3. Determine How Much of Your Savings You Want to Use

Some of you might have savings that you can use to finance the course. In such a case, determine how much of your savings you want to use for the course and how much you want to keep aside as a buffer. I always keep aside at least six months of my monthly expenses just in case I quit my job.

4. Determine How a Salary Cut Will Affect You

More often than not, a career change results in a salary cut. Knowing how much less you earn monthly can help you prepare for the future. If your new income is lower than your current monthly expenses, you will incur a monthly deficit that will eat up your savings. A career change with a monthly deficit cannot be sustained for long.

Expenses > Income = Deficit

If you know a career change will result in a monthly deficit, it is time to cut down on your expenses. Find out what you are spending money on each month and what you spend the most on. Reduce your expenses by cutting away unnecessary expenses, for example:

- Stop buying clothes that you hardly wear.
- End excess insurance plans that you do not need.
- Cut down expenditures on luxury items. They are expenses that you don't need to incur for survival, like travel, meals at expensive restaurants, branded goods, and so on.
- Stop buying things that are not aligned to your goals, like buying unhealthy food when you want to eat healthy.
- Stop buying expensive items and purchase things that can be bought cheaper.

Go through every expense item and ask yourself if you really need to spend your money on it or not: *Is spending money on this more important than your new career or not?* If not, trim it away from your monthly spending. If you want to continue with your current-spending lifestyle, think of other income sources that can supplement your new salary, such as renting out your extra room, getting dividends and capital gains from trading stocks, become a part-time tutor, or earn passive income online.

Question #6: How Much Time Do You Need?

Setting an expected time frame for your career change can keep you moving and help you determine whether or not you are on track.

Ask yourself for the following dates:

- **Registration date:** When do you wish to start your course and when do you need to register?
- **Resignation date:** When do you wish to resign from your current job?
- **Start date:** When do you wish to start your first day of work in your new career?

Before I began my accounting job, I already established a loose time frame for myself:

- First year: I would learn my job scope well and save up money.
- Second year: I would decide on what job I wanted to have and what education I would need to get that job.
- Third and fourth years: I would study the course and acquire the skills I needed.
- Fifth year: I would resign my job and get the job I desired.

I ended up leaving my job a year or so earlier than planned because I needed the time to develop my passions. But it's quite an accurate gauge. The good thing about having a budget and time frame is that it gave me the confidence to pursue my passion earlier. I tend to plan my budget conservatively. As I was doing my monthly budget, I realized my financial status and my spending lifestyle could support my being unemployed for a year or two, so I decided to focus on my animation studies full-time.

To plan out your time frame, do the following:

1. Find Out How Long the Course Is

Courses can be as short as three months to as long as four years, depending on how much skill and qualifications are needed for your new job.

2. Find Out the Payment Plan

Find out if the course fee can be paid in one lump sum or by installments. If payments can be made by installments, find out how frequent each payment is; for example, do you have to pay monthly or quarterly?

3. Determine When You Can Comfortably Start the Course

In general, the number of months you need to save up money before you can start the course can be calculated with the following formula:

$$\frac{\text{Course Fee}}{\text{Monthly Surplus}} - \text{Number of months for the course}$$

The amount of the course fee will be adjusted if you have allocated some savings or borrow some money from your family for the course. For example, if the course fee is $24,000, and you have allocated $4,000 savings to finance this course, then the additional course fee you need to save up for is $20,000.

Let's say your course is 2 years long (i.e., 24 months long) and your monthly surplus is $500. Then, the number of months you need to save up before you can start the course is simply: ($20,000 / $500) - 24 = 16 months.

The above equation is a good gauge when you can comfortably start your course, but it is based on the following assumptions:

- You don't resign before your course ends.
- You have a consistent monthly surplus.
- Your course fee is paid monthly at the end of each month.

If you pay for your course at the beginning of each month, simply add one more month to the final figure. If the course is paid quarterly instead, change the formula to reflect quarters:

$$\frac{\text{Course Fee}}{\text{Quarterly Surplus}} - \text{Number of quarters for the course}$$

So, using the same example, the course is 8 quarters long (24 months / 3 months per quarter). The quarterly surplus is

$1,500 ($500 x 3 months). Then, the number of quarters you need to save up for before you can start the course is simply: ($20,000 / $1,500) - 8 = 6 quarters (rounded up to the next quarter).

4. Run Different Scenarios to Get the Most Favorable Outcome

After I determined when I could start my course, I ran a few different scenarios in excel spreadsheet to keep my options open. (I love doing this.)

If you want to start your course earlier, you can change the variables and see what happens. You can change:

- The monthly surplus (project your salary increment and/or reduce your expenses further)
- The savings allocated for the course fee

Or, you can reverse engineer the results by determining first when you want to start the course. Then, work out how much surplus you need to save monthly for your course. Using the same example previously, if you want to start your course 3 months from now, your monthly surplus will have to be: $20,000 / (24 + 3) = $741 per month, that is:

$$\frac{\text{Course Fee}}{(\text{Number of months for the course} + \text{Number of months you want to start from now})}$$

If you think that you cannot maintain the monthly surplus, you can run another scenario where you decide on the monthly surplus first and see what the course start date will be, that is, see when you can afford to start the course.

The purpose of running different scenarios is just to give you a quick overview of what could happen. It allows you to be flexible. If, after you start your course, you feel like leaving your job to focus on your studies full-time like I did, you can just quickly adjust the variables and evaluate if you can support this change financially.

Plan Loosely and Conservatively

One good practice to follow in planning is to plan loosely. Have rough dates and rough ideas of how much money to set aside each month, but there's no need to follow your plan a 100 percent. **Leave some room for opportunities.**

Inspiration along the way can steer you to a better path. Adjust your plan accordingly in response to unexpected events. Most of the time, life doesn't go according to how you plan it, so don't try to control every single detail. Having a plan just prepares you for the transition and gives you a good gauge of your progress.

Another good practice to follow in planning is to plan conservatively. Envision for the best, but prepare for the worst. When you plan conservatively, it is more likely to meet or even exceed your expectations. I saved a lot more than I needed for my studies when I planned for the worse.

Strategies to Get Your Job

Writing a good resume and applying for jobs through company websites and online job sites are the most basic things you can do to get a job. But they are not enough to get you the job you desire in a competitive job market.

Job hunting is a job.

You have to be proactive and allocate time for it:

- Read books and resources on job hunting.
- Brush up your resume writing and interview skills.
- Find more information on the industry you wish to enter.
- Ask your friends and relatives for job leads.
- Find out hidden or unadvertised vacancies by cold-calling.

Gather anything that helps you prepare for your future career and ask yourself: *What can I do to bring myself one step closer to the career I desire?*

Pay your dues first. Think creatively and develop a long-term strategy to get the job you desire. But at the same time, see what you can do now to get you closer to what you desire.

Here are a few strategies to help you accomplish that goal.

Get into Your Desired Industry First

In his book, *What Color Is Your Parachute?*, Richard N. Bolles says that it's easier for you to first change either your job or your industry to the one you desire instead of changing both at the same time.

When I left my first job as an auditor, it was easier for me to get an accounting job than a creative job. I didn't have much skills and experience in the creative industry yet. So, I became an accountant in a media company (HBO Asia) first to learn more about the industry and its operations before I pursued a creative job. Since I have a background in accounting, I can negotiate for a higher pay compared to what I would make at a creative job.

This is a good method if you don't know exactly what career you want to pursue yet and you need some income to tide you over for the time being.

Focus on Quality, Not Quantity

Job hunting is not about casting your net all over the job market and hoping you catch a job. You don't apply for just any available job. To reap the most out of your job-hunting effort, you need to focus on your job search.

Take the list that you previously completed in "Question #3: Where Are the Jobs You Want?" and target those companies that you are interested in working for. Tailor your resume and cover letter specific to the company's needs. Make it more personal and think in terms of their perspectives.

Also, stay organized and keep track of who you have talked to. When I'm job hunting, I'll prepare a "job control sheet" in an excel worksheet to track all the resumes I've sent and note the dates I've sent the resumes out. I'll check the company website regularly for job openings. Even if there's no opening, I'll still e-mail my cover letter and resume to the company and ask to be considered for future job openings. I'll update the company with a new resume and follow up periodically.

Reach Out to Companies You Want to Work For

In 2009, before I resigned from my auditor job, there was an accountant opening in HBO Asia. I was excited. It was the job I was looking for, an accountant in a media industry. However, I was half a year short in terms of experience as per the job description. I applied for the job through a job agency anyway.

But a couple of days later, someone from the job agency called me and said, "Sorry, you are not qualified for this job you applied for. We will keep you posted if we have other job openings that are suitable for you."

I was bummed.

Another month passed and I resigned as auditor without a job. I was unemployed for a week. Suddenly, I had a brilliant idea.

"Why don't I call up HBO Asia and ask if they need any part-time employees to help them ease their workload? It is the year-end anyway. They are probably busy and need some help."

I was nervous to call the HR department. I had never cold-called and asked for a job before. But I was thinking, "What the heck, at most I get rejected and I don't see them ever again." So, I called up the company and offered myself as a part-time worker.

Thankfully, the company hired me. And after two weeks, I was offered a full-time job for that accountant position that I was "unqualified" for.

***

Starting a new career is tough. You don't have enough work experience. Why would any company take the risk to hire you as a full-time staff member? You have to take the initiative to reduce any risk they feel they face in hiring you. And how do you do that?

You let the company sample your work for free or at very low cost. Volunteer or offer yourself as an intern, part-time, or contract worker. It's a win-win situation. From the employer's perspective, it can see whether you are a good fit for the organization and whether you can pick up the skills fast enough. It lowers the company's risk of hiring a wrong person and increases your chances of getting your job.

> *A good work ethic speaks louder than*
> *a resume or interview.*

From your perspective, you need the experience (and probably the income). Even if the company doesn't hire you, at least you have something to put on your resume now. Perhaps you can request a testimonial from the company, too. Plus, you get to test whether you love the job and the work environment. And, at the very least, it helps to redefine you job search.

Keep Trying until You Receive a Yes

Be Mr. or Ms. Persistent. My persistence helped me to get the accountant job I wanted. Prior to getting the accountant job, there was another opening as an accounts assistant in HBO Asia that I applied for. I made it to the interview, but I was overqualified for the position.

I could have given up at many points in the job-hunting process, being overqualified, unqualified, and uncomfortable in cold-calling. But I didn't. I knew what I wanted and I kept trying. Have a clear goal in mind and keep trying new ways to get it until you receive a yes. You might be just a phone call away from getting the job you desire.

Capitalize on Social Media

In chapter 6, Dan's story is a good example of how you can capitalize on social media to get the career you desire. His website is a resume by itself. It shows he knows how to do marketing, communicate, and get attention to his website.

During my interview with Dan, he mentions that the traditional way of applying for jobs is dead. **You have to do more than you are asked to.** Don't just apply for a job you love with a resume or CV. Go above and beyond. Do something additional that is relevant to your field. Build a website, write a blog, post videos online, or create a Facebook page. Brand yourself with social media. Social media will get you more jobs as compared to a regular application.

For example, if you want to be a mechanic, Dan recommends you set up a YouTube video channel and post videos of yourself showing how to build something. An employer who has two candidates with relatively little experience will choose the one with the videos because he has displayed his skills and ability in the videos. This is also why people who want to sing for a living get so popular through social media. It is a quick way to share your talent and skills.

Using social media not only gets you more attention and showcases your abilities, it also gives you the experience you need for a job.

Increase Your Contacts and Ask Them to Help You

Networking might sound intimidating to you. You have to go out and meet new people and introduce yourself. But it's very effective for job searching, especially when you are doing a career switch. Since you are new to the industry, you won't know many people in the industry. Networking can help you expand your contacts. The more people you know in the industry, the more job leads you will receive.

People also like to work with people they know or friends of people they know. Whenever there were vacancies where I worked, my superiors would ask my colleagues and me for referrals first. It shortens the hiring process and saves the hassle of advertising for the position (not to mention it saves the company money, too). Most jobs are hidden from the public view.

If you aren't comfortable talking with strangers, look to your existing networks first. They include your friends, family, relatives, neighbors, colleagues, and even friends you made online. Your network is anyone you know or strike up a conversation with.

Always let others know you are changing careers. They might just introduce a contact to you. Networking is the same as making friends and building relationships. Don't put too much stress on yourself to find a job this way. Have fun with it.

Deal with People Close to You

Career change can be lonely when you are not getting support from your spouse and parents. When you make a change so drastic like a career switch, people close to you are bound to feel uncomfortable. They are naturally going to bring you back to a place that is familiar to them. And they do that by constantly discouraging you by saying things like:

- You can't do it.
- It's silly to make a career change; you will earn much less than what you do now.
- There's no future in changing your career.
- You're wasting your time and money.

I used to feel the need to defend myself and my passions. I would get easily upset and frustrated when my parents didn't support me. Or I would bicker with my dad when he didn't understand why I favor passion over the things he thought were important to me. What I realized was fighting with others doesn't help the situation at all.

232 Yong Kang Chan

There's no need to be righteous when pursuing your passion. You don't have to justify why pursuing your passion is the right thing to do because there is no right or wrong in pursuing your passion. It's just a matter of choice. *And it's your choice.*

Here's what you can do instead to resolve the tension and tame the unsupportive voices out there.

1. Believe in Your Choice

There's no need to ask others to support you. When you believe in your passion, your commitment and results will convince them one day.

People believe in your ability
when you believe in your ability first.

If you constantly need to convince other people to support you, it just shows them you aren't confident about making a career change. And when they sense you aren't confident, what do they do? They dissuade you from doing it.

It's only when you have doubts will you allow what other people say affect you. Remove any doubts and limiting beliefs you have that tell you that you can't be successful.

2. Listen and Understand Why They Feel this Way

If people you love disapprove or discourage you from pursuing your passion, listen to them but don't react to their comments. People like your parents have your best interests at heart, but they, too have their beliefs regarding what can or cannot be done. And your spouse might feel financially insecure with your career change. Talk to them and understand what they are feeling.

People generally mean well. They have good intentions when they give you feedback, but if they feel their positions are threatened, they might offer critical comments. Their negative comments are nothing personal against you, so don't take them personally.

3. Communicate Clearly to Them

People might not understand why you want a career change. They are involuntarily forced to be part of it, and they are concerned about the impact on their lives. It's your responsibility to communicate clearly how it's going to affect them, so that they can prepare for the change, too. For example, you might not be able to spend as much time (and money) with your friends as you did before. You intend to still see them, but maybe for a cup of coffee instead of an expensive dinner.

Calm them down and reassure them if necessary, but be firm about your career change. If they say something that hurts you, let them know how you feel. If they constantly bring you down, tell them you are not going to stay around to listen to their negative comments. Every time they start criticizing you, walk away from them and don't participate in the exchange. Teach them how you want to be treated.

When All Else Fails...

I added this portion late to the book because it was a recent event, but I wanted to share it with you.

> **News Flash:** I was just offered a six-month contract work as a 3D animator in Malaysia. It's my first animation job and I'm super excited. Hurray!

Then, I told my dad about it and his first comment was: *"What good is that? I don't know what you are thinking."* Ouch! I know what I suggest in this section is easier said than done. But trust me, as you can see by this exchange with my dad, I have been there. Since I was young, I have tried everything to get my dad to understand me a little better, but nothing has seemed to work.

I believe you are born into a family for a reason. I'm here to teach my dad to be more open-minded and positive; he's here to develop my resilience and communication skills. We have different views on life, and we are fated to push each other's buttons. I can't guarantee that he will understand me one day, but I can guarantee that I won't stop pushing his buttons.

So, Malaysia here I come!

Well, when all else fails... take a deep breath, let it go, and move on.

Chapter 12

HOW TO BE PASSIONATE BEYOND WORK

DR SIEW TUCK WAH USED TO BE AFRAID OF DOGS, but now he is a dog rescuer. Growing up in a poor family, Dr Siew never had a pet or much contact with animals. His fear of dogs came from his parents. They would tell him stories of how they were chased and bitten by dogs in the past.

His perception toward dogs only started to change when his partner bought a Japanese Spitz eight years ago. However, it was not till he adopted a stray dog that he developed a deep sense of love and compassion for dogs—in particular, mongrels.

Four years ago, Dr Siew adopted a mongrel from a construction site after he came across her photo on Facebook. At first, he had his reservations. Although the white puppy was very cute, she was rather grey and dirty. And like many people believe (falsely), he thought that mongrels were wild, aggressive, and had diseases.

This mongrel—later named Yoghurt—not only grew up to be beautiful and clever, she in fact ignited Dr Siew's passion for rescuing stray dogs. She changed his initial impressions of mongrels and taught him as well that stray dogs can be loyal and friendly. Through Yoghurt, he realized it was very meaningful and rewarding to save a dog's life.

You Can Always Do More than You Think You Can

So after saving Yoghurt, Dr Siew saved more stray dogs and got them into loving homes. It broke his heart every time he heard stories about how the strays were beaten, chased away, or culled, but there was only so much he could do. He couldn't possibly house all the dogs on the streets!

At least that was what he thought at that time.

In December 2011, the news reported that a female jogger was bitten by a pack of stray dogs in Punggol, Singapore. This incident made the authorities step up their measures in catching and culling stray dogs in that area. Dr Siew felt sad for those innocent stray dogs. Most of them were timid in nature and would not attack people unless they felt that their survival was threatened.

But again, he felt limited. He felt that he could not do anything about the situation. All he could do was to go down to the temple and pray for the dogs to be safe. That day, as he was praying in front of Guanyin, the Goddess of Mercy, he felt an overwhelming compassion for the dogs and started crying uncontrollably. At that moment, he received a strange thought:

"Call the media and contact the lady who was bitten by the dog."

This sign from above was an awakening for Dr Siew—he realized he could possibly do something about the situation. So he followed the sign given to him and called the media. Even though the lady refused to talk to him, the local news picked up on the story. Eventually, he and other dog lovers gathered to start a movement to save the Punggol strays. They managed to rescue more than fifteen dogs from death.

The following month, the dog welfare group Save Our Street Dogs (SOSD) approached him and asked him to head their committee. He gladly accepted and embarked on his mission to save more street dogs in Singapore.

His Passion for Rescuing Dogs Changed His Life

As an aesthetic doctor, Dr Siew used to focus a lot on appearances and glamour. Pursuing wealth and branded goods used to be his highest priority in life. But after he was involved in rescue work, several things changed for him.

- He became more grounded and realized that nothing is more important than life.
- He sold his Audi and bought a Toyota instead with the intention to help expand the shelter.
- His entire lifestyle changed. He now prioritizes rescue work over less meaningful activities like partying and playing Mahjong.
- He is so busy now that he has less time to meet his friends. Because of that, he lost some friends, but he

gained new friends who share the same passion for dogs.

- He understands his patients a whole lot better now and develops a closer relationship with them. Many of his patients became his friends and ended up being volunteers for SOSD.

- He became passionate about Buddhism and practices mediation frequently now.

"When you deal with life and death all the time, it changes you."

Doing something he loved transformed him in more ways than he could have imagined. He felt very fortunate to find his passion in rescuing stray dogs. Not only did he have the power to create change, he experienced positive changes within himself.

Key Lessons from Dr Siew's Story:

1. Pursuing passion transforms you.

Dr Siew's initial intention was just to save lives. He did not expect himself to lead a welfare group or have the power to change the public's perception toward stray dogs. He had never run an organization or a business before. Activities such as facilitating a meeting, liaising with different people, and managing a team were not part of his normal routines as an aesthetic doctor. Pursuing his passion provided him the courage and the opportunity to learn these leadership and management skills.

More importantly, his compassion for the stray dogs created an internal shift within himself. His priorities in life changed, he appreciates life more, and now he is content with what he has.

Everyone has a different passion. Sometimes passion is given to you for a special reason — to help you grow as a person.

2. Fear can be easily changed to love.

Don't you find it ironic that the things that we are the most afraid of are often things that are unfamiliar? Dr Siew's fear of dogs was a result of not having any contact with dogs. His fear was solely based on his parents' experiences, not his. Once he was able to spend time with dogs and had a better understanding of them, his fear just evaporated into love.

This also applies to our fears when it comes to pursuing our passion. We have fears because we lack knowledge about our passion. We are not sure how to pursue our passion. We are uncertain of the challenges and obstacles we are going to face. But all these fears can easily disappear once you take actions and gain more knowledge about your passion.

3. You can always make time for passion.

Initially, it was very difficult for Dr Siew to juggle time between his work and his passion. Rescue work took up a lot of his free time. There were a lot of meetings to attend, calls to respond to, and sites to visit. Furthermore, his day job required him to work six and a half days a week.

However, he was able to work around it. First, he talked to his bosses and they understood what he was doing and gave him better hours. For example, he gets to leave early on

Friday afternoon to hold SOSD meetings. Secondly, as SOSD expanded, they were able to get more people on board to be volunteers. The new volunteers really helped to share his workload. Lastly, he had a great team that worked like a corporation. The team broke into smaller groups according to their area of specialty and held meetings on their own.

Dr Siew is a good example of someone who makes time for his passion. Not only does he have a challenging job that he loves, he also finds time outside work to pursue his passion in dog rescue and Buddhism. It is all about prioritizing what is more important to you.

Schedule Time to Be Passionate

Passion shouldn't be limited to only your career. Make every waking hour of your life fun, meaningful, and interesting. Adopt a passionate lifestyle. You can start with thirty minutes a day, but remember to schedule it. People easily lose track of time. Scheduling a time for your passion allows you to commit and block off a period of time for it. It's also easier to let other people know you are busy and not to disturb you for that duration.

Having a schedule for passion has other benefits, too:

- If you are a workaholic and find yourself spending too much time at work, having a schedule reminds you to break away from your work and do something else you are passionate about.

- If you are doing random stuff like surfing the web aimlessly, having a schedule makes you conscious of time and stops you from further wasting it.
- If you always feel overwhelmed and like you don't have enough time, having a schedule forces you to choose and prioritize work that is important to you.

Be Creative with Your Passions

Passion should not be taken too seriously; be creative and play with it. Try something you have never tried before, or set new goals with your existing passion. I have a group of friends who love to sing, and we frequently sing karaoke. One day, instead of singing the songs we usually choose for ourselves, I suggested we pick songs for each other to sing.

Playing with your passion has certain benefits:

- **It opens your passion to a wider scope.** My friends and I got to listen to many new songs we previously had not heard of.

- **It challenges you.** We got to learn new songs and try new genres of songs that we had not tried before or did not dare to try.

- **It breathes new life to your existing passion.** We got to pick songs for others to sing, songs that we imagined what they would sound like if another person sang them. It made singing more interactive and fun.

You get more out of your passion when you get creative with it. If you love cooking, instead of cooking Western cuisine all the time, explore other cuisines like Asian or fusion. Make desserts instead. Experiment with different ingredients. Trying new recipes makes cooking more fun.

Pursue Your Passion Outside of Work

There're so many things you can do outside your job. You need not quit your job to pursue your passion. You can pursue it as a hobby. Who knows, your hobby might become handy to you or your career one day. **Be prepared before the opportunity comes.**

Here are some ideas that might help you to pursue your passion outside of your day job.

Volunteer

Join an organization or a cause you are passionate about. If you love animals, join a community that helps animals. If you love to bake cookies, why not bake some for a charity you love? Not only will you get to pursue your passion, you get to interact with others, create new relationship, and give back to society.

Travel

I make sure I travel at least once a year. I'm always inspired when I travel. It widens my perspectives and gives me a lot of ideas. You might have noticed that I've used a few examples from my trip to the United States last year in this book.

There's so much to explore in another country, and every time you explore it in a different way, you get new experiences. Visit new places you have not been to. Try new restaurants. Stay in different hotels each time you go back to the same country. You can also infuse your passion into your itinerary. If you are passionate about photography, traveling is the best time to take tons of cool photos. If you love technology, visit the local IT fairs or stores. You can also interact with the locals who share similar passions as you.

Learn

Learning a new skill is fun. You become a beginner and start from ground zero again. You also get to understand how the things you love are made and appreciate them more. When I study music and animation, I learn how different people contribute to the final product and how much thought is involved to make it good. That makes me love music and animation even more.

But sometimes, people don't want to learn new skills because they are afraid they can't pick them up. They fail to see the joy of learning. Don't learn skills just to advance your career. Learn them for fun. Whether you're good at it or not is not important at all. What's important is to be in the learner's mentality.

Create

Create something new. Begin at home first. Look around your house and see where you can spice things up. Decorate or redecorate your house; add new things to it. Don't just buy them, but also make them using used items you have at home. Look for inspirations and ideas online.

If you are not an artsy person, reorganize your cupboards and wardrobe instead. If you love to build things, improve your home by fixing the old stuff, like my dad does. He will use old furniture, tear it apart, buy new materials, and rebuild them from scratch again.

If you love to use computers, why not design new wallpaper for your computer? If you love family gatherings, organize an event for your family. Create a new outing. Don't do the same routine. For example, instead of just having a meal together all the time, organize a BBQ instead. There are so many things you can do and create with your passions.

Share

If you love photography, share your photos online with others. Create a blog. Talk in forums. You can always find people who have the same passion as you do. Don't be limited by your geographical location. Build a community and make friends all around the world. Share knowledge with one another and help each other out. You might just form a business partnership with someone online and create something great.

Be Inspired to Inspire

Passion is fueled by a series of inspirations and taking actions. It is a nonstop cycle. Your passion gives you inspiration to act. **You decide to act on your inspirations or not.**

When you act on your inspirations, you create more of the things that you are passionate about. These things you created will, in turn, inspire you to continue to do more of what you love. The cycle goes on and you keep your passion burning. (See Figure 12.1.)

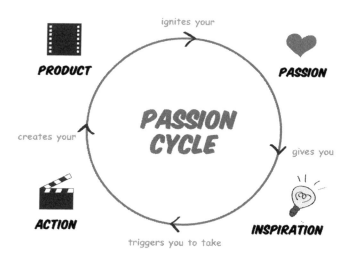

Figure 12.1 Passion is a nonstop cycle if you choose to act on it.

Sometimes, others get inspired by you along the way. For example, you watch a movie that you love or a documentary show on filmmaking and you feel inspired to make your own short film. So you take the action to create a simple short film and post it online. Watching your film makes some others feel it's possible to make a short film, too. They are inspired and go ahead to make their own. And the cycle goes on.

Taking action on your passion is like paying it forward. When you do what you love, you are going to inspire more people to do what they love. The whole Universe will benefit from your decision to act.

FINAL THOUGHTS

Reading this book is only the beginning. Zig Ziglar, an author and motivational speaker, once said that those who don't take step number 1 will not take step number 2. I congratulate you for taking the first step toward your passion by reading this book.

More importantly, I hope you will take actions on your passion. Sometimes, people get a lot of ideas after reading books, but they end up not doing anything at all. I hope you do implement some of the stuff in this book.

Pace yourself. Take it slow. Don't implement all your ideas at once. Some methods and suggestions in this book might not suit you and that's okay. Just move on to the next one. Even if you can't find anything that is applicable to you, I hope this book at least opens up your perspective to what passion can bring you and inspires you to explore your passion.

Remember, you deserve the best.

Have fun and live a passionate life. Enjoy every bit of your passion. Continue to discover what your passions are and instill them in every aspect of your life, regardless if you are at work, at home, or with others. No matter how tired you are, passion will find a way to put a smile on your face.

Finally, whenever you have doubts about your life, ask yourself:

Did I do something I love today?
If not, why not?

ACKNOWLEDGMENTS

I WOULD LIKE TO THANK my parents for taking care of my needs so that I could pursue my passions. Thanks to my mum for providing me with lunch and dinner when I wasn't working. Thanks to my dad for fixing my computer every time it didn't work so that I could continue with my writing. He drove me to work every morning, even when I was working part-time at HBO Asia!

More importantly, I would like to thank my parents for not nagging me too much when I left my job as an accountant. I knew they didn't agree with my decision and didn't understand what I was doing with my career, but I want to thank them for having faith in me and accepting me as the passionate son I am.

I'm also grateful for all the help and ideas I received from my two wonderful brothers. It's great to have creative siblings who I can bounce ideas off of and get valuable feedback from.

This book would not be published without the help of Steve Harrison's wonderful team: Geoffrey Berwind, Martha Bullen, Brian Edmondson, Raia King, Mary Giuseffi, and Deb Englander. It has been a joy and a pleasure to work with everyone. Special thanks to Geoffrey and Martha who helped me a lot in storytelling. I will definitely use the things you have taught me in my future books and blog posts.

And let me not forget Mishael Patton from Ann McIndoo's team. Thank you for motivating me in the beginning. I wouldn't have drafted the outline of this book as quickly if it weren't for you.

I would also like to thank all my friends who had encouraged me and given me positive feedback for my blog posts. Your support gave me the courage to write this book and made me believe I could do this. I'm also grateful for everyone who did my initial survey. Your feedback helped me better focus my writing.

To my dearest HBO colleagues: I'm never coming back to work as an accountant! But seriously, I loved working with all of you. Thank you for always welcoming me back with open arms.

To all the friends I made in Animation Mentor, it's a blessing to know so many passionate people around the world. Passion is infectious. So stay passionate! I'm coming to join you all in the world of animation. A big thank you to the founders: Bobby, Shawn, and Carlos for creating such an awesome school. I'm blessed to have found the school.

Lastly, to all my readers, thank you for reading this book. By reading this book, you allow my voice to be heard.

Thank you very much!

STORY CONTRIBUTORS

HERE'S A SPECIAL THANKS to all the contributors who shared their stories. Thank you for taking time out to do the interviews. I learned a lot from our interviews together. Thank you for inspiring the readers (and me) with your stories.

Chapter 2 - Simon Gudgeon

Simon Gudgeon is one of Britain's leading contemporary sculptors. He has attained worldwide recognition with exhibitions in London, New York, San Diego, Paris, and the Netherlands. Sculpture by the Lakes at Pallington in Dorset provides a tranquil backdrop for his monumental finished pieces and houses convenient studio workshops. See more of his work at:

http://www.simongudgeon.com/

Chapter 3 - Larry Jacobson

A California native, circumnavigator and adventurer Larry Jacobson is a recognized entrepreneurial and leadership expert. An avid sailor, he has over 50,000 blue water miles to his name. Author of the award-winning bestseller, *The Boy Behind the Gate*, and author of the new audio program, *Navigating*

Leadership for Entrepreneurs, Larry is a motivational speaker and entrepreneur coach. He lives in the San Francisco Bay Area and welcomes new clients and inquiries at:
http://larryjacobson.com

Chapter 5 - Peter Yang

Peter Yang is the founder of Empact. Based in Singapore, he has extensive experience in advising social enterprises and nonprofit organizations in realizing their missions. Empact empowers them by providing them access to affordable and professional services that are critical to their daily operations. Find out more at:
http://www.empact.sg/

Chapter 5 - Swami Sadashiva Tirtha

Swami Sadashiva Tirtha (The Hip Guru™) is the author of the amazon #1 bestselling Ayurveda Encyclopedia, and spoken at the White House Commission on Complementary and Alternative Medicine Policy. He is a breakthrough expert helping colleges & companies reduce their stress quickly and with joy. Swamiji is a monk, teaching meditation & yoga since 1977, and integrative healing since 1988. See more details at:
http://TheHipGuru.com

Chapter 6 - Dan Conway

In 2013, Dan Conway branded himself as "The Extreme Job Hunter" and launched a viral media campaign to get a job. His campaign was featured on the news both locally and nationally in the UK. He now works at Vitamins Direct doing what he loves. You can see the publicity stunts from his campaign at: http://www.theextremejobhunter.com/

Chapter 8 - TaJuan "TeeJ" Mercer

Residing in North Hollywood, CA, TeeJ Mercer is an award-winning TV Editor, International Bestselling Author, and highly sought-after speaker. Her storytelling mastery takes audiences on a journey every time she speaks. TeeJ is raw, transparent, and amazingly authentic. Plus, she is the absolute best hugger! She can be reached at: TeeJ@TheRealityTVCoach.com

Chapter 10 - Leanne Spencer

Leanne Spencer is a Personal Trainer and fitness entrepreneur based in London, UK. Aside from her business interests, she is a keen runner and boxer, and practices yoga twice a week. She lives in London with her partner and two cats, and is working on her first novel in her spare time. You can reach her at: http://www.bodyshot-pt.co.uk

Chapter 11 - Anne Rupert

Anne Rupert was born in the Netherlands. After receiving an MA in Modern English Literature, she worked for a large UK housing group for 10 years. In 2014, she started a six-month career break, working for free to develop her skills and gain inspiration. She is recording her experiences in: http://www.callofthewildgeese.com

Chapter 12 - Siew Tuck Wah

Siew Tuck Wah is an aesthetic doctor based in Singapore. He is currently heading the nonprofit group, "Save our Street Dog" (SOSD). SOSD focuses on advocating for strays and assisting the integration and acceptance of mongrels in society. Their mission is to give street dogs a chance in life. Find out more at: http://www.sosd.org.sg/

ABOUT THE AUTHOR

YONG KANG CHAN, best known as Nerdy Creator due to his popular blog of the same name, is a former accountant who is currently pursuing his passion in animation. Based in Singapore, he is also an award-winning songwriter who loves being creative and helping creative people be successful in their life. Learn more at: www.fearlesspassion.com.

Made in the USA
Las Vegas, NV
07 June 2021